Lamp of Mahamudra

Lamp of
Mahamudra

Lamp of Mahamudra

*The Immaculate Lamp
That Perfectly and Fully Illuminates
The Meaning of Mahamudra,
The Essence of All Phenomena*

Tsele Natsok Rangdröl

Foreword by
Kyabje Dilgo Khyentse Rinpoche

Introduction by
Kyabje Tulku Urgyen Rinpoche

Translated from the Tibetan by
Erik Pema Kunsang

Rupa & Co

First edition, 1988
Second edition, 1989, Shambhala Publ., Boston
Third editon, 1997

First in Rupa Paperback 2004

Published by

Rupa . Co

7/16, Ansari Road, Daryaganj,
New Delhi 110 002

Sales Centres:

Allahabad Bangalore Chandigarh Chennai
Hyderabad Jaipur Kathmandu
Kolkata Ludhiana Mumbai Pune

ISBN 962-7341-25-8

By arrangement with
Rangjung Yeshe Publications

This edition is for sale in the Indian sub-continent only.

Printed in India by
Saurabh Printers Pvt Ltd,
A-16, Sector-IV, Noida 201 301

Dedicated to the swift return of
Kyabje Tulku Urgyen Rinpoche

Dedicated to the swift return of
Kyabje Tulku Urgyen Rinpoche

Contents

Foreword

The most learned Tsele Pema Legdrub was the body-emanation of the great translator Vairochana, and he attained the pinnacle of learning and accomplishment of the masters of the Land of Snow. Also known as Kongpo Götsang Natsok Rangdröl, he was unmatched in his three qualities of scholarship, virtue, and noble-mindedness.

Among the five volumes of his collected works, I considered that this *Lamp of Mahamudra* would benefit everyone interested in the dharma. The words are clear and easy to understand, and lengthy scholarly expositions are not emphasized.. This text, easy to comprehend and containing all the key points and very direct instructions, results from following the oral advice of a qualified master.

In order to help the foreigners who are presently interested in the dharma to gain true confidence, I, old Dilgo Khyentse, encouraged my disciple Erik Pema Kunsang to translate this book into English. Therefore, may everyone trust in this.

Written on the twenty-fifth day of the first month of the year of the Earth Dragon.

DILGO KHYENTSE RINPOCHE

Translator's Preface

Lamp of Mahamudra is the second of three renowned books by Tsele Natsok Rangdröl being translated by the order of Venerable Tulku Chökyi Nyima Rinpoche. This edition was published for the eighth yearly seminar on Buddhist theory and practice at Rangjung Yeshe Institute, Boudhanath, Nepal.

The following autobiographical information about Tsele Natsok Rangdröl was extracted by His Holiness Dilgo Khyentse from the inner life story of Jamgön Kongtrul the Great recounting the succession of his past incarnations:

The most learned master Tsele Pema Legdrub Natsok Rangdröl was prophesied as the body-emanation of the great translator Vairochana. Renowned as the reincarnation of the incomparable Tendzin Dorje, he was invited to the Thangdruk Monastery, established by his previous incarnation. Attending numerous learned and accomplished masters, including Gangra Lochen, he fully comprehended the philosophical scriptures and oral instructions of sutra and tantra, according to the new and old schools. Being extremely disciplined, even the liquor in his feast offerings was prepared from water with molasses. Besides this his tongue never touched a drop of alcohol.

In the later part of his life he stayed in Palri Götsang, the cave of Deshek Tse in the south, and

other places where he perfected the realization of
mahamudra and dzogchen. Among his disciples
are included Gampopa Sangpo Dorje, Bomting
Chöje Miphampa, Tau Pema Lodrö, and others.

I would like to thank Marcia Binder Schmidt for acting
as the translation assistant, checking all stages of the work,
Judith Amtzis for her repeated editing, as well as John
Rockwell and Wayne Amtzis for their useful suggestions.

ERIK PEMA KUNSANG
Nagi Gompa, Nepal
1988

Introduction

SUMMARY OF MAHAMUDRA

Mahamudra has three modes: sutra mahamudra, mantra mahamudra, and essence mahamudra. Sutra mahamudra is attaining the stage of complete buddhahood through traversing the five paths and ten bhumis.

Mantra mahamudra is experiencing the four joys via the third empowerment, which lead to the four levels of emptiness. The four types of joy, supreme joy, nonjoy, and innate joy lead one to the means for realizing the ultimate view of mahamudra. In the traditional statement "to reach the true wisdom by means of the symbolic wisdom," the symbolic wisdom refers to the four levels of emptiness invoked by the four joys, while true wisdom is mahamudra of the natural state. Introducing mahamudra of the naked, natural state in this way is called mantra mahamudra.

Essence mahamudra is described in terms of essence, nature, and expression. The essence is nonarising, the nature is unobstructed, and the expression is what manifests in manifold ways. Essence mahamudra is pointed out through skillful means as follows: "Essence mahamudra is your naked, ordinary mind resting in unfabricated naturalness."

Although the teachings on essence mahamudra and dzogchen of the natural state use different terminology, in actuality they do not differ at all. Through such teachings, the mind at the time of death merges with dharmakaya the instant that the material body disintegrates. It is also possible to attain true and complete enlightenment in the dharmadhatu realm of Akanishtha while still remaining in this physical body.

This state of mahamudra is the flawless realization of all the learned and accomplished masters of India without exception, the six ornaments and two supreme ones as well as the eighty mahasiddhas. Simply hearing the word "mahamudra" leads to the end of samsaric existence.

As the great master Trangpo Tertön Sherab Öser wrote:

> Mahamudra and dzogchen
> Differ in words but not in meaning.

In terms of ground, path, and fruition, ground mahamudra is the nonarising essence, unobstructed nature, and expression manifest in manifold ways. The dzogchen teachings describe these three aspects as essence, nature, and compassion.

Path mahamudra is naked, ordinary mind left to rest in unfabricated naturalness.

Fruition mahamudra is the final seizing of the dharmakaya throne of nonmeditation. The four yogas of mahamudra are called one-pointedness, simplicity, one taste, and nonmeditation. The stage of fruition is realized when the dharmakaya throne of nonmeditation is attained.

One-pointedness, the first yoga of mahamudra, has three levels: lesser, medium, and greater. One-pointedness, for the most part, consists of shamatha and the gradual progression through the stages of shamatha with support, without support, and finally to the shamatha that delights the tathagatas. During this process fixation gradually diminishes.

The next stage, simplicity, basically means nonfixation. During the three levels of lesser, medium, and greater simplicity, fixation falls more and more apart. While one-pointedness is mainly shamatha, simplicity emphasizes vipashyana.

One taste is the state of mind in which shamatha and vipashyana are unified. Appearance and mind arise as one taste. One does not need to confine appearances to being there and consciousness to being here, but the dualistic fixation of appearance and mind mingle into one taste in the space of nonduality.

When in retreat at Gampo Mountain, Lord Gampopa told one of his disciples, "The mingling of appearance and mind is like this!" As he simultaneously moved his hand freely through the room's main pillar, the upper and lower parts of the pillar disconnected, not touching each other. The caretaker was later frightened and thinking the roof would fall down, he placed a piece of slate between the pillar sections. Gampopa's act was an expression of reaching the greater level of one taste, the stage at which the world and beings, all dualistic phenomena, mingle into one taste in the space of nonduality. Dualistic concepts such as good and bad, pure and impure, pleasure and pain, existence and nonexistence, objects to be accepted or rejected, adopted or avoided, as well as hope and fear: everything intermingles as one taste, the royal seat of dharmakaya.

At this level there still might remain some sense of enjoying the spectacle of one nature, one taste, but at the fourth stage, nonmeditation, even subtle concepts of watcher and something watched, meditator and object of meditation, are dissolved within the space free from mental constructs. Thus, the dharmakaya throne of nonmeditation is attained. Dzogchen calls this stage the exhaustion of phenomena beyond concepts. Nothing needs to be meditated upon or cultivated; that is dharmakaya.

Introduction

At the time of one-pointedness don't fixate.
During simplicity don't fall into extremes.
Don't cling to the taste of one taste.
Nonmeditation transcends conceptual mind.

Here I have given a short and comprehensive outline of
mahamudra.

TULKU URGYEN RINPOCHE
Nagi Gompa, Nepal
1988

Lamp of Mahamudra

PROLOGUE

Namo Mahamudraye

Perfectly pure since the beginning,
The nature is devoid of all fabricated attributes.
This supreme and luminous wisdom of dharmata
I worship with the homage of realizing it as it is.

Though no existence is present in the essence itself,
Its manifest aspect has the magic of manifold ap-
    pearance.
I shall now explain so you can recognize your
    nature,
This natural mode of innate inseparability.

The quintessence of the meaning of all the infinite and countless teachings of the buddhas is that the wisdom essence of the tathagatas is present as the nature of sentient beings. The innumerable different kinds of dharma teachings and vehicles are indeed only taught for the purpose of realizing this nature. There are as many gates to the dharma and types of instructions that tame as there are different kinds of inclinations and talents of those to be tamed. This is due to the special and wondrous power of the compassionate activity of all the buddhas.

Among all these different kinds of teachings is one that is the most eminent, the shortest path, the ultimate mean-ing of the summit of all the vajra vehicles of the resultant secret mantra. Renowned like the sun and the moon, mahamudra is the supreme method that directly and easily

1

Prologue

reveals the natural face of mind in which the three kayas are spontaneously present. It is the one highway journeyed by all supreme siddhas and vidyadharas. I shall now explain the necessary points of its meaning briefly in three sections:

1. Ground mahamudra, the essential nature of things; the meaning of the view, briefly stated in terms of confusion and liberation.
2. Path mahamudra, the self-existing natural flow; the manner in which the paths and bhumis are traversed, explained extensively in terms of shamatha and vipashyana.
3. Fruition mahamudra, the manner in which the welfare of beings is accomplished through the realization of the immaculate and ultimate three kayas of buddhahood; explained as the conclusion.

SECTION ONE

GROUND
MAHAMUDRA

THE VIEW

Ground mahamudra, the essential nature of things. The meaning of its view, briefly stated in terms of confusion and liberation.

Your natural essence cannot be established as either samsara or nirvana. Not confined by any one extreme, free from the limitations of exaggeration and denigration, it is neither tainted nor spoiled by such designations as pleasant or unpleasant, being or not being, existent or nonexistent, permanent or annihilated, self or other, and so forth. Because it is not established as a certain kind of identity, your essence can serve as the basis for the manifestation of any form or conception to manifest. Yet, no matter how it manifests, ultimately this essence has no true existence. Thus, it is a great emptiness free from the limitations of arising, dwelling, and ceasing—the unconditioned dharmadhatu. Since the beginning it is a nature in which the three kayas are spontaneously present, and it is known as the "ground mahamudra of the essential nature of things." The *Guhyagarbha Tantra* teaches:

> This mind-essence devoid of ground and root
> Is the basis of all phenomena.

This essence is not something that exists within the mind-stream of just one individual person or just one buddha. It is the actual basis of all that appears and exists, the whole of samsara and nirvana.

5

When you realize its nature, cognizing its actual condition, you are called a buddha. When you do not realize it, remaining ignorant of it and experiencing confusion, you are called a sentient being. Thus it serves as the basis for wandering in samsara and is known as the general ground of samsara and nirvana. The Great Brahmin Saraha stated:

This single mind is the seed of everything.
From it, samsaric existence and nirvana manifest.

It is a single essence with different manifestations or with different aspects appearing, simply due to the difference between having or not having realized it. Whichever of these two occurs, it still abides as the great primordial indivisibility of the three kayas with neither good or bad nor any defect such as changeability tainting its essence. The general vehicles call this the "unchanging absolute." It is also the primordial ground nature.

This nature present as a neutral and undetermined ground, neither realized nor not realized, is known as the "all-ground," "alaya," because it forms the basis for both samsara and nirvana. This all-ground, not a mere nihilistic and void nothingness, is self-luminous cognizance that occurs unceasingly. That cognizance, called "all-ground consciousness," is like a mirror and its brightness.

THE BASIC SPLIT

Now follows an explanation of how the split between samsara and nirvana arose from this single all-ground.

As for the cognizant quality or wisdom aspect of this self-luminous consciousness, its essence is empty, its nature is cognizant, and these two are inseparable as the core of awareness. Being the seed or cause of all the buddha qualities and attributes of the pure paths, this is also known as the "true all-ground of application," "sugata-essence,"

"dharmakaya of self-cognizance," "transcendent knowledge," "buddha of your own mind," and so forth. All
these names given to the classifications of nirvanic attributes are synonymous. This wisdom aspect is exactly what
should be realized and recognized by everyone who has
entered the path.

Due to the ignorant aspect of this neutral all-ground,
you do not cognize your own essence, and the natural
state is not realized. In this way have you obscured yourself. Called "coemergent ignorance" or the "great darkness of beginningless time," since it is the basis from
which all disturbing emotions and deluded thoughts arise,
it is also known as the "all-ground of various tendencies."
Hence it is the ground of confusion of all sentient beings.
The *Openness of Realization Tantra* explains:

> Since awareness did not arise from the ground,
> This completely mindless oblivion
> Is the very cause of ignorance and confusion.

Accompanying this ignorance are also the seven thought
states resulting from delusion, such as medium desire and
forgetfulness.

From this coemergent ignorance arises a fixation on an
ego and self-entity. On the basis of this "self" arises the
fixation on "other." Not recognizing this personal manifestation for what is, a personal manifestation, one grasps
at it as though it were an external object. This onset of
confusion through not recognizing the nature of the
thoughts of fixation on perceiver and perceived is called
"conceptual ignorance" or "mind consciousness." It is the
cognitive act of confusing object and mind as being separate and is accompanied by the forty thought states resulting from desire, such as attachment and clinging.

From the expression of this mind consciousness, various

kinds of tendencies and confusions will arise and unfold. Aiding that, through the power of the solidifying force of dependent origination, such as the condition of the all-pervasive wind of karma and the cause of the ignorant aspect of the all-ground, the body, appearances, and mind are fully formed. The different sense consciousnesses of the five sense-doors and the manifestation of perceptions and thoughts of the six collections are also called the "dependent."

The five major root pranas and the five minor branch pranas provide the vehicle for the thoughts. Through the power of being habituated to confused fixation, your personal manifestations will appear as a world with inhabitants. Based on this foundation and its objects, everything is produced. Also known as the "defiled mind," it is what moves through the different five sense-doors, creating attachment and so forth. Therefore it is also called the "consciousnesses of the five senses." Accompanying it are also the thirty-two thought states resulting from anger, such as medium detachment and so forth.

In that way, the all-ground of various tendencies as the root and the eighty inherent thought states as the branches gradually grow, and confusion becomes continuous. Through this you wander endlessly in samsara. That is the way of confusion of unrealized sentient beings.

Because of that confusion, the tendencies of all the phenomena of samsara and nirvana remain in this all-ground in the manner of seeds. The various objects of gross materiality and the pure and impure parts of nadi, prana, and bindu of the inner body, as well as all the various phenomena of samsara and nirvana, the worlds and beings of the three realms, appear externally in an interdependent manner. All of these, however, like objects appearing in a dream, are a magical display of superficial appearances, which do not actually exist. Growing more and more used to fixating on them as being permanent, solidifying and clinging to them as being real, you experience the various kinds of pleasure, pain, and indifference of the three realms and six classes of beings. You spin perpetually through the causes and effects of samsara as though on the rim of a water wheel. The general characteristics of sentient beings are indeed like this.

HOW THE ESSENCE REMAINS

Although confused in this way and wandering in samsara, the nature of the sugatagarbha, your essence of awareness, has become neither impaired nor decreased even in the slightest. The *Taknyi Tantra* says:

> All sentient beings are buddhas,
> But they are covered by temporary stains.

In the ultimate sense, this primordial nature is vividly present as the inseparable three kayas. Moreover, even when obscured by the temporary stains of deluded experience, this natural face of the essence is still vividly present as the three kayas. Finally, it is also vividly present as the three kayas at the time of realizing the fruition, when what obscures has been cleared away and when the twofold knowledge is perfected. For this reason, the duality of confusion and liberation is simply a label given to the mere state of not being free from the stains of deluded thinking and ignorance. The *Uttara Tantra* declares:

> Just as it was before, so it is afterward.
> It is the changeless nature.

Although the nature of mind is spontaneously perfect as the primordially pure essence, this temporary confusion or coemergent ignorance through which you have obscured yourself originated from yourself, like an impurity covering gold. Various means of purifying and cleansing these obscurations have been taught. This essence, which itself is self-existing wisdom, unchanging throughout the three times, and devoid of conceptual constructs, is the actual knowledge aspect. All the paths can therefore be included under "means and knowledge." That is the ultimate realization of the victorious ones.

You might think, "Isn't it illogical that the single all-ground explained above should split into both samsara and nirvana?" In fact, it resembles the medicine camphor, which causes either benefit or harm depending on whether a sickness stems from heat or cold. Moreover, a single poisonous substance that will normally cause death can become medicine if utilized by some skillful means such as a mantra. Similarly, you are liberated when you are aware of and recognize the single nature of the all-ground and deluded when ignorant of the all-ground and apprehending it as a self-entity. Thus, the all-ground is only changed by realizing or not realizing. Noble Nagarjuna has taught:

> Covered by the web of disturbing emotions,
> One is then a "sentient being."
> Freed from disturbing emotions,
> One is called "buddha."

For this reason, embracing all phenomena with the skillful means of the mahamudra instructions of the essential true meaning, you will attain stability in the nature of ground mahamudra. You will purify the impurities of confused thought by path mahamudra and capture the royal throne of the three kayas, which is fruition mahamudra. Thus, you will open up for the treasure of the twofold benefit. A karmically destined person who is a

worthy recipient should therefore search for a truly qualified master endowed with the nectar of blessings, and one
should follow him according to the example of how Sadaprarudita followed Manibhadra or how Naropa followed
Tilopa. You should definitely have your being ripened by
either extensive or condensed procedures of ripening empowerments, the main entrance door to the path of vajrayana. Then you should exert yourself in each and every one
of the general and special preliminaries until some signs
manifest, without giving in to comfort-seeking, indo-
lence, or belittling the practice. This is to be highly
treasured as the beginning guidance of the liberating instructions.

In particular, through the richness of devotion to your
master, you should emphasize practicing without hypoc-
risy. Furthermore, you should be sure to receive the
warmth of his blessings. This is the sacred essence of the
the tradition of all accomplished Kagyu vidyadharas. The
Great Pacifying River Tantra declares:

> This coemergent wisdom, beyond description,
> Is recognized only through the practices of gath-
>   ering accumulations and purifying one's veils
> And through the blessings of a realized master.
> Know it to be delusion if you depend on other
>   means.

Now comes the main part itself. No matter which style
of teaching one follows according to the traditions of
practice of the different lineages—recognizing the meditation from within the view or establishing the view from
within the meditation—the exclusively important chief
point is to receive the blessings of the lineage masters.

THE ACTUAL VIEW

In general, the different vehicles and the various philosophical schools have countless ways of accepting a view,

and each in essence has a true, established basis. Since all the vehicles are the infinite display of the all-encompassing modes of activity of the victorious ones, I will not describe them with such words as pure or impure, good or bad, but only rejoice in them.

In this context, the view is the mind-essence—spontaneously present since the beginning as the great and total purity. Free throughout the three times of past, present, and future, from the constructs of arising, dwelling, and ceasing, as well as of coming and going, this mind-essence is unspoiled by the conceptual attributes of fixating on samsara, nirvana, and the path. It is not exaggerated or denigrated as existence or nonexistence, being or not being, permanence or annihilation, good or bad, high or low. It transcends refutation and proof, accepting and rejecting, changing and altering any of all the appearing and existing phenomena that comprise samsara and nirvana.

The exact nature of this original state or mode of being is totally free in being inseparable appearance and emptiness and vividly clear in being the unity of luminosity and emptiness. It is utterly open in being all-pervasive primordial freedom and completely even in being unconditioned spontaneous presence. This is the main body of the view, the natural state as it is, primordially self-existing and originally present as the essence of all of samsara and nirvana. There is no other separate piece or fragment of a view than this.

To see the inherent falsity in dualistic fixation through understanding this primordial condition is called "realizing the view," and also "seeing the mind-essence" or "cognizing the nature of things." As described in the *Doha Kosha*:

The View

When realized, everything is that.
No one can realize anything superior.

In actuality, all of appearance and existence, samsara and nirvana, is the display of the three kayas. Your own mind as well has the nature of the three kayas and itself is not apart from ultimate dharmadhatu. All samsaric attributes are contained within the mode of the mind's characteristics. All attributes of the path are contained within the mode of the dharma. All attributes of fruition are contained within the mode of the mind's capability.

The nonarising essence of the mind itself is dharmakaya, its unobstruced expression is sambhogakaya, and its function manifesting in any way whatsoever is nirmanakaya. These three kayas are again spontaneously present as an indivisible identity. To recognize and settle on this natural state is called perfectly realizing the faultless and correct view. A view different from this—a view or meditation imputed through intellectual concepts of assumption or through attributes of reference such as being free or not free from extremes, high or special, good or bad, and so forth—has never been taught as the view of mahamudra.

SECTION TWO
PATH MAHAMUDRA

SHAMATHA AND VIPASHYANA

The meditation of path Mahamudra. Explaining shamatha and vipashyana, faults and qualities, meditation and postmeditation, misunderstandings, how to traverse the path, and so forth.

The term "meditation" and the ways of meditating in the context of each of the numberless philosophical schools generally have numerous meanings; but here the word "meditation" is merely given to the act of acquainting mind with the meaning of the natural state, the view as explained above. You never meditate by fabricating something mentally, such as a concrete object with color and shape. Nor should you deliberately meditate while suppressing the mind's thinking or perceptions, as in meditation on a constructed emptiness. Meditation means simply sustaining the naturalness of your mind without any fabrication.

In particular, there are various kinds of mental capacities and intelligence. People with sharp faculties, the instantaneous type who are realized through former training, can possibly be liberated simultaneously with recognizing their essence, with no need to be guided gradually through shamatha and vipashyana. But other, ordinary types of

17

people must be guided gradually. Therefore, begin with training yourself in the stages of shamatha with attributes, by focusing on a stick, stone, deity image, or syllable; or train in the practices of prana and bindu and so forth. Having attained confidence in these practices, then engage in the supreme shamatha without attributes.

SHAMATHA

The actual shamatha meditation is taught through the following three meditation techniques:

1. Not letting the mind wander after any outer or inner object, rest in undistracted freshness.
2. Not controlling your three doors by being too tight, rest freely in effortless naturalness.
3. Not letting the essence of a thought and the wakefulness be separate and different as if applying an antidote, rest in the natural clarity of self-aware self-cognizance.

Other names, such as "nondistraction," "nonmeditation," and "nonfabrication," are also used for these three.

The three gates of emancipation taught in the general vehicles are contained within these three as well: The mind itself refraining from following after one's actions or what happened concerning past actions and events is called the "emancipation gate of marklessness." Your present mind, free from mind-made tampering and construction or the negating and affirming acts of "Now this appears! This is what I should do!" is itself the "emancipation gate of emptiness." Being free from anticipating that such and such is to occur in the future, as well as being free from desire and yearning, such as hoping that meditation will happen or fearing that it will not, is the "emancipation gate of wishlessness." These are, in short, included within simply letting your mind rest in naturalness—unspoiled and without fabrication.

When a thought suddenly manifests in that state, simply vividly recognizing your essence without following after what occurs is sufficient. Do not try deliberately to inhibit it, to concentrate inwardly in meditation, or to control it with some other remedy. Whatever action of that type you might take is not the vital point of sustaining the mind-nature in uncontrived nonfabrication.

Although other paths contain various teachings about this, the context here has only the path of recognizing the essence of whatever occurs; if you search for some other technique it will not be the meditation of mahamudra. As the Great Brahmin declared:

> The meditation of all beings is spoiled by effort.
> While there is nothing at all to be meditated upon,
> One should also not be distracted for even an instant.
> This I proclaim, is the meditation of mahamudra.

By thus resting evenly in the nature of mind as it is, the three experiences of shamatha will gradually manifest. What are they? At first, the mind seems more agitated, with even more thought activity than before. Sometimes between thought activity, your mind remains still for a short while. Do not regard such thought activity as a defect. Although up to now your mind has been always thinking, you did not recognize that. This point, of recognizing the difference between thinking and stillness, is the first shamatha experience, like the waterfall on a mountain cliff.

After maintaining the practice like that, the thoughts will be mostly controlled. You become gentle and relaxed; both your body and mind become totally blissful and you do not feel like engaging in other activities, but only delight in meditation. Except on rare occasions, you remain mostly free from any thought activity. That is the intermediate shamatha stage, like the gentle flowing of a river.

Later on, after practicing with undistracted endeavor, your body becomes totally blissful, free from any painful sensation. Your mind is clear cognizance free from thoughts. Not noticing the passing of day and night, you can remain unmoved for as long as you are resting in meditation, and you are unharmed by faults. The manifest disturbing emotions have subsided, and you have no strong clinging to such things as food and clothing. You have conditioned superknowledges, and various kinds of visionary experiences occur. The manifestation of these numerous kinds of ordinary qualities is the final state of shamatha, which is like an unmoving ocean.

Many meditators, who at this point do not connect with an experienced master and who have great diligence but little learning, become infatuated with these seemingly good qualities. Also, ordinary people see them as siddhas, and that leads to the danger of creating disaster for both self and others. So be careful.

This endeavor in shamatha meditation does not qualify as the main part of mahamudra practice, but it is certainly essential as a foundation. Gyalwa Lo-re has said:

Dull shamatha without clarity
You may meditate on for a long time without
    realizing the nature.
Possessing the gaze with sharp awareness,
Meditate by continuing short sessions.

THE VIPASHYANA OF THE MAIN PART

Without completely clarifying doubts about resolving whether or not the nature of your mind has any concrete

attributes, such as shape or color and so forth, whether it
has a place of origin, dwelling, and departure, whether it
arises and ceases, whether it is existent or nonexistent,
permanent or annihilated, or whether it has a center and a
limit, you will be unable to arrive at the view as it truly is.
Lacking that, you will not know how to sustain the
meditation naturally and spontaneously. Not knowing
that, regardless of how much deluded shamatha and per-
severing mind-fixing you may do, you will not transcend
the cause and effect of the three realms of samsara. You
should therefore clear away your misconceptions in the
presence of a qualified master.

In particular, the secret mantra being the path of blessings, you should exert yourself in the means for assimilat-
ing the realization of the lineage masters' blessings. By
doing that, you will directly experience your own awareness which, as explained above in the context of the view,
is spontaneously present since the very beginning as the
essence of the three kayas. You will experience it as a direct
and nonconceptual wakefulness, which does not fall into
any of the extremes of existence or nonexistence, eternalism or nihilism. Although experienced and understood as
being cognizant, aware, empty, and inseparable, this
wakefulness cannot be illustrated by analogies, and it
transcends any means of expression through words. This
state of being—wide awake in self-existing and natural
cognizance—is indeed what is called vipashyana.

First of all, ordinary people have never, for even a single
instant, been separate from this natural cognizance. Yet,
because of not having embraced it with oral instructions
or blessings they have not recognized it. Next, this natural
cognizance is what remains in shamatha and what observes
whether or not there is stillness or thinking. It is the doer
of all these things. Yet, it is like not seeing yourself. The

21

projection of a train of thought by an ordinary person is nothing other than vipashyana itself manifesting as conceptual thinking. Moreover, the experiences of shamatha as well as bliss, clarity, and nonthought are nothing other than the vipashyana awareness manifesting as such experiences. But because of not recognizing your naked essence free from concepts, these experiences have become a mere sustaining of stillness and not the cause for enlightenment. After you have recognized your own essence, there is not a single state, be it stillness or thinking, which is not vipashyana or mahamudra. Lorepa clarified this:

When you are not involved in mental fixation,
Whatever manifests as the objects of the six
    collections,
Everything is self-liberated personal experience.
Have you realized this inseparability, you
    meditators?

THE UNITY OF SHAMATHA AND VIPASHYANA

Shamatha is generally held to mean abiding in the state of bliss, clarity, and nonthought after conceptual thinking has naturally subsided. Vipashyana means to see nakedly and vividly the essence of mind, which is self-cognizant, objectless, and free from exaggeration and denigration. In another way, shamatha is said to be the absence of thought activity, and vipashyana is recognizing the essence of thought. Numerous other such statements exist, but, in actuality, whatever manifests or is experienced does not transcend the inseparability of shamatha and vipashyana. Stillness and thinking both are nothing but the display of the mind alone; to recognize your essence at the time of either stillness or thinking is itself the nature of vipashyana.

22

Shamatha is not to become involved in solidified clinging to any of the external appearances of the six collections, while vipashyana is the unobstructed manifestation
of perception. Thus within perception the unity of shamatha and vipashyana is complete.

Vividly recognizing the essence of the thought as it
suddenly occurs is shamatha. Directly liberating it within
natural mind, free from concepts, is vipashyana. Thus
within conceptual thinking shamatha and vipashyana are
also a unity.

Furthermore, looking into the essence without solidly
following after a disturbing emotion, even when it arises
intensely, is shamatha. The empty and cognizant naked-
ness within which the observing awareness and the ob-
served disturbing emotion have no separate existence is
vipashyana. Thus the unity of shamatha and vipashyana is
complete within disturbing emotions as well.

SUMMARY

The essence of your own mind does not exist as stillness
or thinking, projection or dissolution, good or bad. All
phenomena that appear are merely the unobstructed manifestation of the display of your mind. Similarly, shamatha
and vipashyana themselves have no existence other than as
an indivisible unity. However, so that people can easily
understand, their manifestation has been taught under
different names and classifications.

Shamatha alone has therefore been stated to be ineffec-
tive as the main part of mahamudra meditation because:

> Stillness alone is the mundane dhyana.

The dhyanas of the non-Buddhist tirthikas and even the
Buddhist dhyanas of the shravakas and pratyekabuddhas
as well as the samadhis of all the god realms are ordinary.

They are therefore not the actual path of the fourth empowerment of mantra. In particular, in mahamudra clinging to the experience of stillness is inadmissible. Mahamudra is the occasion for practicing what appears and exists as being dharmakaya. If one accepts stillness as good, as being meditation, and rejects thinking as bad, as not being meditation, that does not accord with appearance and existence being dharmakaya, or with leaving whatever occurs free from fabrication.

FAULTS AND QUALITIES

Having briefly discussed the meaning of shamatha and vipashyana, I shall now explain something about faults and qualities, as well as the different kinds of purpose.

The two parts are: In general, the explanation of the mistake of not understanding how to sustain resting in equanimity; and in particular, the explanation of how to clear away the faults of the different types of errors and deviations.

EXPLANATION OF MISTAKES

Resting one's mind without fabrication is considered the single key point of the realization of all the countless profound and extensive oral instructions in meditation practice such as Mahamudra, Dzogchen, Lamdre, Chö, Shije, and so forth. The oral instructions appear in various modes due to the difference in ways and capacities of human understanding.

Some meditators regard meditation practice as simply a thought-free state of mind in which all gross and subtle perceptions of the six senses have ceased. That is called straying into a dull state of shamatha.

Some presume stable meditation to be a state of neutral dullness not embraced by mindfulness.

Some regard meditation as complete clarity, smooth bliss, or utter voidness and cling to those experiences.

Some chop their meditation into fragments, believing

25

the objective of meditation to be a vacant state of mind between the cessation of one thought and the arising of the next.

Some hold on to such thoughts as, "The mind-nature is dharmakaya! It is empty! It cannot be grasped!" To think, "Everything is devoid of true existence! It is like a magical illusion! It is like space!" and to regard that as the meditation state is to have fallen into the extreme of intellectual assumption.

Some people claim that whatever is thought or whatever occurs is of the nature of meditation. They stray into craziness by falling under the power of ordinary thinking.

Most others regard thinking as a defect and inhibit it. They believe in resting in meditation after controlling what is being thought and tie themselves up in fixated mindfulness or an ascetic state of mind.

In short, the mind may be still, in turmoil as with thoughts and disturbing emotions, or tranquil in terms of the experiences of bliss, clarity, or nonthought. Knowing how to sustain the spontaneity of innate naturalness directly in whatever occurs, without having to fabricate, reject, or change anything, is extremely rare. It seems necessary to have a faultless practice in harmony with the actual statements of realization in such texts as the sutras and tantras of definitive meaning as well as the collected works, oral instructions, and guidance manuals of the lineage of accomplished masters.

CLEARING AWAY SPECIFIC ERRORS AND DEVIATIONS

All the forefathers of the Practice Lineage having taught this in detail and extensively, I shall here explain the errors simply, as a brief indication.

Clinging to any of the three experiences of bliss, clarity,

or nonthought while resting in meditation will create the causes for rebirth in the three realms of desire, form, and formlessness. Being reborn there, you will, when your life span ends, again fall down into the lower realms. Thus, they are not the path to buddhahood.

Dividing up this topic in detail, there are in particular the nine dhyanas of absorption. When resting evenly in shamatha, then, to be free from gross thoughts of perceiver and perceived but still to be fettered by the concept of meditator and meditation object is called the "samadhi of the first dhyana." Why is that? Because this is what is being meditated upon in all the abodes of the gods of the first dhyana. Meditating in this way creates the cause for being reborn there as a god at the level of the first dhyana.

Likewise, the second dhyana is to be free from the state of mind of concept and discernment, but still to experience the taste of the samadhi of joy and bliss.

The third dhyana is to be free from mental movement, but supported merely by the inhalation and exhalation of breath.

The fourth dhyana is to be free from all kinds of thoughts, a state of samadhi that is unobstructed clarity, like space.

Supreme among all the mundane samadhis, these are the foundation for vipashyana. If meditated upon with attachment, however, they become a deviation from mahamudra, causing rebirth as gods in the abodes of those dhyanas.

Furthermore, one might think "All phenomena are infinite like space!" or "This consciousness, free from partiality and nonexistent, is infinite!" or "Perception, being neither existent nor nonexistent, is not an action of mind!" or "This mind is voidness, which is nothing whatsoever!" Dwelling in the states of these four levels has the defect of straying into the four formless spheres of finality, called the "infinite space," "infinite consciousness," "neither presence nor absence," and "nothing whatsoever."

The shravaka's samadhi of peace is the state of mind that has abandoned these four thoughts, in which involvement in objects has been blocked, and in which you abide having interrupted the movements of the prana-mind. Although such a state is taught to be the ultimate shamatha, in this context it is not a faultless meditation unless embraced by vipashyana.

Each of these nine dhyanas of absorption has some temporary qualities, such as the accomplishment of superknowledges and miraculous powers. Here, however, you should attain the ultimate result of complete enlightenment and not merely relative or superficial qualities. Thus, if these are accomplished naturally and you then cling to them or feel arrogant, know that to be a direct obstacle for enlightenment.

THE EIGHT DEVIATIONS

Having explained these errors and ways of going astray, I shall now teach the eight deviations:

1. Not understanding that the mind-essence is the unity of appearance and emptiness endowed with the supreme of all aspects, the unobstructed interdependence of cause and effect, you slip into focusing on the empty aspect. Acknowledge this fault called "basic straying from the essence of emptiness."

2. Similarly, after engaging in meditation, although you may have merely intellectually understood the meaning of the natural state, experience has not arisen in yourself. Or, again forgetting that which has arisen, the meaning will not be present within your being, although

you might be able to explain the words to others. That is called "temporary straying from the essence."

3. While what is needed at present is the path itself, you desire to attain some other result later on. That is called "basic straying from the path."

4. To regard the sustaining of the ordinary wakefulness of your mind as insufficient while you desire a magnificent mind-made meditation and then search for it elsewhere is called "temporary straying from the path."

5. When something such as a disturbing emotion arises, not to know how to take its essence as the path and instead to meditate on some other technique according to the lower vehicles is called "basic straying from the remedy."

6. Not knowing how to take whatever arises, such as a thought, as the path, but to block off that instance or having to destroy it before resting in meditation is called the deviation into the "temporary straying from the remedy."

7. Not understanding that the natural state of the mind-essence is primordially empty and rootless and fabricating such thoughts as "It does not possess a self-nature!" or "It is emptiness!" or "It is just temporarily empty!" is called "basic straying into generalized emptiness."

8. Thinking, "Formerly I was distracted following after thoughts, but now I am meditating nicely!" and then remaining in the state of perpetuating that thought, or, thinking that you have mindfulness when you do not and so forth is called "temporary straying into generalizing."

SUMMARY

Not recognizing the key point of the natural state and not resolving doubts about how it actually is, you risk straying into these and various other kinds of incorrect, look-alike meditations. Exertion in an incorrect, look-alike meditation for no matter how long is fruitless. Some people create the causes and conditions for an evil state, such as being reborn as a naga by meditating on shamatha cessation. You must therefore have an unmistaken meditation.

Moreover, some people regard a dull or sluggish state of mind free from thoughts as shamatha. They presume that vipashyana means analyzing with thoughts. They believe that a solid and rigid fixing of the mind is mindfulness and mistake a state of neutral indifference for the natural. They confuse the ordinary mind of a commoner, who has not seen the original face of the natural state, for the innate ordinary mind free from fabrication. They regard the clinging to a good samadhi or the mere conditioned bliss of being free from pain as the innate supreme bliss. They mistake the involvement in clinging to apparent objects without having attained the certainty of recognizing the objectless natural state for the unobstructed self-cognizance that is free from object and fixation. They confuse the stupidity in which cognizance is blocked for being nonconceptual wisdom and so forth.

In short, all the different types of mistakes, incorrect look-alikes, strayings, and deviations are primarily caused by not having applied onself fully to the key points of the preliminaries, such as gathering the accumulations and purifying the obscurations. Hence, the defilements of negative karma have not been cleared away. Next, not having treated yourself with the ointment of blessings, your mind is uncured and inflexible.* Not having resolved your doubts in the main part of the practice, you have become insensitively caught up in theory and absorbed in words. Finally, not having taken the practice to heart, you have

---

*Just as cowhide, uncured by oil, is rigid and unpliable.

become a person with a dharmic exterior who is neither a practitioner nor a lay person and who ruins the teachings of the Practice Lineage. There are many of that kind in this final end of the dark age. The *Seven Wheels of Kshiti-garbha Sutra* states:

> Not accepting the cause and effect of the ripening
>   of karma,
> One is a non-Buddhist proponent of nihilism
> And is reborn in the Avichi hell right after dying.
> It will ruin others and destroy oneself.

You must therefore exert yourself intelligently and not become like that.

EXPERIENCE AND REALIZATION

Endeavor one-pointedly to rest in equanimity without falling prey to mistaken or deluded views and meditations, and without going astray or deviating. Also, embrace the ensuing understanding with mindfulness, without remaining in the confused dissipation of ordinary abandonment. You will then have some experience and realization in accordance with the particular type of person you are or your degree of mental capacity.

In general, due to the many different systems of the various learned and accomplished masters, numerous different ways of identifying these experiences and realizations have appeared. Some say, however, that among the four yogas, after reaching simplicity there is no actually separate meditation or postmeditation. Some make the division into a different meditation and postmeditation for each experience and realization respectively. Some teach a different meditation and postmeditation for each of the individual stages of the four yogas. Innumerable different ways indeed exist.

Similarly, there are various systems concerning the differences between experience and realization. Some have taught that the three levels of one-pointedness are only experience and not actual realization. The different teachings appear to have countless details, such as accepting that the mind–essence is seen at the time of having reached nonmeditation and so forth.

Experience & Realization

Since all these teachings are compassionate manifestations intended as means to tame the infinite number of inclinations, dispositions, and frames of mind of people, respectfully speaking, you need not regard one teaching as the exclusive truth. I, myself, have not reached, perceived, or understood all these stages. So how can I set down any maxims as to what is the case and is reasonable or that such and such is not the case and is unreasonable? That would be like a person born congenitally blind who cannot distinguish between beautiful and ugly colors. Based on my own degree of understanding, however, I shall now describe these stages in brief.

MEDITATION AND POSTMEDITATION

The terms and examples for meditation and postmeditation are present during all cultivations of the two stages. The two stages of vajrayana practice are the development stage and completion stage. How is that? The word "meditation" means to focus on the actual thing to be practiced without mixing it with other activities, and the word "postmeditation" means to mingle it with other activities, such as during practice breaks. The state of mind at that time is called "ensuing understanding," and perceptions are termed "ensuing perception." In general all systems designate them like this. Also, in this context, one can call it "meditation" when beginners are exerting themselves in the actual meditation practice and "postmeditation" when one is doing things such as walking, moving about, eating, sleeping, and so forth. For the eminent practitioners, meditation and postmeditation are inseparable; always free from distraction and confusion, their practice is continuous.

EXPERIENCE AND REALIZATION

As for the distinction between experience and realization, "experience" refers to a certain virtuous practice of

33

any high or low level which is not mingled with the essence of mind and which includes something to be relinquished and its remedy. Or one can say that experience is to retain the concept of a separate meditator and meditation object. "Realization" means that the virtuous practice and mind are not separate, but manifest as the essence of mind, which is resolved in the attainment of certainty. In short, these two aspects appear not only in the context of actual meditation but also refer to most of the practices of the path, such as guru yoga, compassion and bodhichitta, development stage, and so forth.

The following example describes this. Having heard from others a rough idea or the story about Vajrasana, when its shape and scenery appear in your mind and you can explain it to others, this is called "intellectual understanding." Approaching Vajrasana from a distance or looking at a drawing of its architectural outlines so that your mind comprehends its approximate meaning is called "experience." Having gone to Vajrasana yourself, looked at it carefully, and felt certain about it is called the arising of "realization."

THREE TYPES OF PEOPLE

Whether or not these points are easily comprehended depends upon the mental capacities of individual people. These can be divided into three degrees. People who give rise to understanding, experience, and realization by merely being shown a symbol or who, in one instant, quickly perfect the qualities without having to exert themselves through hardship are called the "instantaneous type." These are great beings who have realization through former training. People whose qualities of experience and realization increase and decrease without sequential order or without being fixed as high or low are called the "skipping the grades type," those with middling capacity. Other general or ordinary people of the type who ascend in definite progressive stages, according to their degree of diligence, are called the "gradual type," which includes all ordinary people. Since the former two can also be included within the progressive stages of the path conforming to the gradual type, I shall here explain according to the gradual way.

THE FOUR YOGAS

The common vehicles teach that one journeys to buddha-hood through the ten bhumis and five paths. But here I shall explain the four gradual stages of yoga particularly famed among the lineage masters of the incomparable Dakpo Kagyu. These four yogas, each divided into lesser, medium, and higher stages, resulting in twelve, are the meaning nature of the scripture called the *Tantra of the Inconceivable Secret*, elucidated by Lord Dawö Shönnu. That tantra teaches:

> By the samadhi of the majestic lion,
> Your clear mind of immovable one-pointedness is
>   radiant.
> It awakens self-cognizant wisdom from within,
> And with stable *acceptance* you abandon the suffer-
>   ing of the lower realms.
>
> By the second, the samadhi of magical illusion,
> Out of the great meditation of simplicity,
> Appears the inconceivable as the power of samadhi.
> And having attained the *heat,* you gain mastery
>   over rebirth.
>
> By the third, the samadhi of courageous move-
>   ment,
> Multiplicity being one taste, the realization of the
>   ten bhumis manifests.
> You accomplish the benefit of others as a son of
>   the victorious ones of the three times,

And having attained the *summit,* your progress is uninterrupted.

By the fourth, the vajralike samadhi,
One of endeavoring in the practice of nonmeditation,
Your wisdom knowledge perceives the buddha realms.
Effortlessly and spontaneously present, it is the great state of the *supreme attribute.*

These stages and their corresponding meaning are extensively described in the *Lankavatara Sutra* as well. Acharya Shantipa likewise has elucidated this in great detail through explaining the five eyes, omniscience, and so forth. Moreover, according to the mahamudra system of the Nyingma tradition, Guru Rinpoche has also taught their meaning concisely. In the *Nekyi Sintig* he describes one-pointedness:

With virtue and evil purified in the mind
You automatically relinquish nonvirtuous actions.

Simplicity:

With mind-essence free from mental constructs
You relinquish all fixations of perceiver and perceived.

One taste:

With appearances arising as dharmakaya
You automatically relinquish conceptual thinking.

And nonmeditation:

By recognizing samsara and nirvana to be devoid of self-nature

You relinquish all dualistic fixations.

Thus, he taught the four yogas combined with the four exertions. Furthermore, Guru Rinpoche taught:

> Heat is to see the nature of mind.
> By summit you realize nonarising as dharmakaya.
> Through acceptance you transcend rejecting samsara and adopting nirvana.
> Supreme attribute is samsara and nirvana dissolving into mind.

This teaching combines the four yogas with the four aspects of ascertainments on the path of joining, the meaning of which corresponds with the above.

THE FOUR YOGAS

As just a humble indication, I shall now explain the progressive way in which the actual meaning of these four yogas manifests and, in addition, how the ten bhumis and the five paths of the sutra system are perfected.

Among one-pointedness, simplicity, one taste, and nonmeditation, first is the yoga of one-pointedness:

One-Pointedness

When a worthy person who has cut attachment to this life and who perceives his master as a buddha in person has received genuine blessings and then rests in evenness, he abides in the states of bliss, clarity, and nonthought and acquires certainty. To retain the fixation of thinking, "Meditation is the self-liberation of arising thoughts through recognition" is the lesser one-pointedness.

Although the forefathers of the Practice Lineage regarded the three stages of one-pointedness as only shamatha, according to my own understanding there must of course be different levels of people. Furthermore, for someone who has recognized the innate state, the nature of things is that shamatha and vipashyana are always present as a unity. Therefore, understand that here shamatha is embraced by vipashyana. The ensuing understanding at this point is dominated by fixation on solidity, and during the dream state you are also not much different from an ordinary person. In short, since at this time you are a beginner, you have various kinds of highs and lows in the ease or difficulty of maintaining the practice.

At the time of the medium one-pointedness, you can remain in the meditation state for as long as you desire. At times, samadhi occurs even without having meditated. The ensuing understanding grows less fixated on solidity so that perceptions become wide open, and virtuous practice sometimes occurs during sleep as well. It is, in short, the time of meditation becoming meditation.

Following that comes the greater one-pointedness. Throughout day and night the meditation state becomes an uninterrupted experience of bliss, clarity, and non-thought. Without divisions into ensuing experience, ensuing understanding, and so forth, your samadhi becomes continuous. You are free from outer or inner parasites and do not become involved in clinging to sense pleasures. It is taught that you will also attain some superknowledges and miraculous powers. Up to this point, however, you are not free from the experiences of clinging to something excellent and are not liberated from the fetter of conceptual mind fixating on meditation.

Numerous differences exist in the levels of capacity of those who have begun these three stages of one-pointedness, as well as in the individual degree of their diligence. That is to say, whether or not you have seen the essence of one-pointedness is said to depend upon whether or not you have attained the confidence of self-cognizance within the states of bliss, clarity, and nonthought. Likewise, the difference between whether or not you have perfected the training lies in the difference between these experiences being continuous or occasional. Whether or not thought arises as meditation depends upon whether or not all arising thoughts become meditation by merely being embraced by mindfulness. Moreover, the arising of qualities depends upon whether or not your mind-stream has become pliable. The sowing of the seed of the rupakaya depends upon whether or not unfabricated compassion arises during the ensuing understanding. The difference between mastering or not mastering the relative lies in whether or not you have achieved certainty in the dependent connection of cause and effect. These are the measurements taught by the Kagyu forefathers.

Simplicity

Having given rise to some extent to these experiences of one-pointedness, if you exert yourself in supplication and practice, without falling prey to the faults of self-centered arrogance or clinging to something excellent, you will ascend to simplicity. In other words, you will realize correctly that the natural state of your mind-essence is free from the extremes of arising, dwelling, and ceasing. During the ensuing understanding, you are liberated when, having embraced that state with mindfulness, it turns into the state of meditation. However, if not embraced with mindfulness, your postmeditation state becomes fixation on solidity. During dreams it is also uncertain whether or not you are confused. In any case, the lesser simplicity is when you retain some fixation on emptiness, such as thinking, "All phenomena of appearance and existence are nothing but emptiness!"

At the time of the medium simplicity, this fixation on emptiness and the clinging to the nature of thoughts as being real have been purified. Your clinging to outer appearances as being real, however, is not completely eliminated. During the ensuing understanding and during sleep, deluded fixation and clinging to solidity alternate between being present and absent, and you undergo numerous fluctuations in your spiritual practice as well.

The greater simplicity is having completely cut misconceptions about samsara and nirvana, outer and inner, appearance and mind, and so forth. Thus, you are liberated from clinging to "perceived" or "not perceived," "empty" or "not empty," and so forth. Daytime meditation is for the most part uninterrupted, while deluded fixation sometimes occurs during dreams. However, mindfulness has not yet become continuous, so a slightly deliberate mindfulness is necessary. In short, during these stages of simplicity, because you mainly experience emptiness and have the experience of not fixating on anything whatsoever as being real, your devotion, pure perception, and compassion may decrease. Not falling prey to the obstacle of emptiness rising as an enemy is thus vitally important.

At this point, seeing the essence of simplicity depends on whether or not the defilement or conviction of experiences that fixate on emptiness have been purified. The perfection of the training depends upon whether or not you are free from hope and fear or have cut through your misconceptions concerning what is perceived and what is empty. Whether or not thoughts have arisen as meditation depends upon whether or not the realization of the meditation state of recognizing the natural face of all thought occurrences as being nothing but emptiness occurs during the ensuing experience and sleep. The arising of virtuous

41

qualities depends upon whether or not you are connected with the manifest aspect of signs of accomplishment, such as the twelve-times-one-hundred qualities of perceiving the truth, that which is to be realized. Mastery over the relative and the sowing of the seed of the rupakaya depend upon whether or not you can arrange the coincidence of bodhichitta and aspiration after having attained certainty in how the manifestation of emptiness arises as cause and effect. It is taught that you should know these dividing points.

One Taste

After having perfected the realization of simplicity, you understand that designations and distinctions of dualistic attributes such as samsara and nirvana, appearance and emptiness, development and completion, relative and absolute, and so forth all are of one taste in mahamudra. Although you are able to condense all the possible attributes of the path into self-cognizance, as long as you retain a slight fixation on this experience or some attachment to a conviction about self-cognizance, it is called the lesser one taste.

Having purified the fixation on this experience, you attain the realization of appearance and mind as being inseparable, not even fixating on a separate existence of an actual object to be realized and of the awareness that realizes it. Thus, the medium one taste is liberation from the duality of perceiver and perceived.

By the power of the multiplicity of all phenomena appearing as one taste, the expansion of the great expression of wisdom, the realization of one taste itself manifesting as multiplicity, is the greater one taste.

All the forefathers of the Practice Lineage have taught that the genuine mingling of meditation and postmedita-

tion occurs at this point. In other words, any appearance
or thought arising is, from the aspect of its essence,
primordially dharmakaya or mahamudra. But in the aspect
of its manifestation or as it appears to a deluded person it
still retains such characteristics as solid existence and sub-
ject-object fixation. It is in fact self-liberated the moment
it is embraced by self-cognizant mindfulness, a quality not
present in the lower yogas.

The moment of embracing a thought with mindfulness
in this context means simply allowing whatever manifests
or occurs to arise without having to be mindful of or to
recognize some essence separate from that. This happen-
ing depends on whether or not the essence of one taste has
been seen. Whether or not the training is perfected lies in
whether a subtle clinging to an antidote remains or
whether one taste has arisen as multiplicity. "Thought
arising as meditation" depends upon whether or not the
perceptions of the six senses occurring unimpededly have
transcended bondage and liberation. The arising of qualities depends upon whether or not wisdom knowledge has
attained mastery over all outer and inner phenomena and
has acquired the power to make apparitions, transformations, and miracles. Mastery over the relative depends
upon whether or not the coincidence of realizing one taste
arising as multiplicity through the mingling of appearance
and mind, the cause and effect of mastering appearance
and existence, has been brought onto the path. The sowing
of the seed of the rupakaya depends upon whether or not
the treasury of benefit for others has been opened through
the power of all-embracing and effortless compassion.
Many such statements have been made.

Nonmeditation

When after this you have perfected one taste, dualistic
experiences, such as deliberately meditating or not medi-

tating, being distracted or undistracted, are purified, and you are liberated into the great, primordial state in which all experiences are meditation. Lesser nonmeditation, however, is the arising of merely subtle and illusory fixation and tendencies during the night as well as during the ensuing experience.

Medium nonmeditation is when this illusory fixation is utterly purified, after which the continuity of day and night becomes a single great meditation state, and thus the innate nature is realized. But the presence of a subtle aspect of consciousness as self-cognizance, the inherent cover of wisdom, is itself the defilement of dualistic knowledge. So, not being free from that is the medium nonmeditation.

When this lack of recognition of nonthought, this subtle obscuration of dualistic knowledge that is like a remnant of the all-ground consciousness has been completely purified, the luminosity of mother and child mingle together, and everything ripens into an all-encompassing expanse of wisdom, the single sphere of dharmakaya. This, the greater nonmeditation, also called perfect and complete buddhahood, is the arrival at the ultimate fruition.

Seeing the essence of nonmeditation is nothing but the simple realization of what has become evident at the stage of one taste, and therefore depends upon whether or not the mind experiencing an object of meditation or familiarization has been purified. Perfecting the training of nonmeditation depends upon whether or not all defilements of ignorance, the most subtle tendencies of dualistic knowledge, have been exhausted in the wisdom of realization. Thought arising as meditation depends on whether or not the tendencies of the all-ground have dissolved into the state of dharmadhatu wisdom. The arising of qualities depends on whether or not materiality is manifest as or liberated into the rainbow body, mind into dharmakaya, and the realms into all-encompassing purity. Actualization of the seed of rupakaya depends on whether or not the inexhaustible adornment wheel of body, speech, and mind effortlessly accomplishes the welfare of beings throughout space. The purification of all aspects of relative phenomena into dharmadhatu depends upon whether the supreme qualities of buddhahood have been perfected. The Kagyu forefathers have indeed elucidated these and other distinctions.

SUMMARY

As for the meaning of the above condensed into its essence, one-pointedness means being able to remain in meditation for as long as you desire. Simplicity means recognizing your natural face as ordinary mind and realizing it to be devoid of ground and root. One taste means that the dualistic fixation of samsara and nirvana is liberated within awareness. Nonmeditation means that all defilements of conviction and habitual tendencies are purified. The essence of the four yogas is included within this.

In particular, the distinction between the meditation and postmeditation of one-pointedness lies in abiding and not abiding. The distinction between the meditation and postmeditation of simplicity lies in being or not being mindful. Beyond one taste, meditation and postmeditation are intermingled; so there is no distinction.

Moreover, the nature of thought arising as nonthought is one-pointedness, arising as emptiness is simplicity, arising as equality is one taste, and arising as transcendence of conceptual mind is nonmeditation.

Furthermore, at the time of one-pointedness, confusion arises uncontrolled; at simplicity it is realized as devoid of ground and root. At the time of one taste, confusion dawns as wisdom; and the stage of nonmeditation is beyond the words confusion and non-confusion.

It is further taught that the highest achievement at the time of one-pointedness is realizing the inseparability of stillness and thought occurrence. For simplicity, the highest achievement is realizing the inseparability of confusion and liberation. For one taste, it is realizing the inseparability of appearance and mind. And for nonmeditation, it is realizing the inseparability of meditation and postmeditation.

Moreover, it is taught that one-pointedness is when your mind is grasping at solidity; the state of mind of simplicity is meditation and postmeditation; the state of mind of one taste is unity; and nonmeditation is when your mind is realized.

Lastly, at the time of one-pointedness thoughts are subdued; at the time of simplicity the root of thoughts is cut; at the time of one taste self-existing wisdom dawns from within; and nonmeditation is the attainment of stability.

Briefly, the different types of distinctions and classifications are certainly of an inexpressible and inexhaustible number, but the definite key point of utmost importance is as follows. Having recognized the innate mode of mind, the natural state exactly as it is, the fact of knowing how to sustain the spontaneous way of ordinary mind, naturalness unspoiled by mental fabrication, is alone important. The wisdom dakini Niguma said:

> If you don't understand that whatever appears is
>   meditation,
> What can you achieve by applying an antidote?
> Perceptions are not abandoned by discarding them,
> But are spontaneously freed when recognized as
>   illusory.

THE FIVE PATHS AND
THE TEN BHUMIS

Most people nowadays pretending to be dharma practitioners are chained tightly by the bonds of the eight worldly concerns and, merely pursuing material things and the gain of further possessions, have no thought other than for the food, clothing, and pleasures of this life. Some intoxicate themselves with the poison of pride, boasting of a vast learning and knowledge of words but fail to gain mastery over their own minds. Some do aspire toward practicing the definitive meaning but lack an authentic master and the genuine oral instructions. Hence, they imprison themselves within a rigid meditative asceticism— not knowing the practice of all-pervasive openness. Many ignorant meditators earn themselves the prize of soglung.

In these times, when mountains and valleys are filled with so-called meditators who perpetuate misdeeds and lack substance, like a *lung* stew, or are hollow, like a blacksmith's bellows, one may expound upon the qualities of the four yogas, but it will amount to nothing more than telling about the qualities of water in the desert. There is not much point in that.

The fortunate men and women who have definitely given rise to flawless experience and realization do not depend on external words and letters when the knowledge resulting from meditation has arisen from within. Therefore, they surely have no need for lengthy explanations from someone like myself, which are like narrations of a place far away by a person who has not been there himself.

A well-gifted and qualified person, who has given up concerns for this life, who is endowed with perseverance, who follows a perfect master and, having received the blessings, can practice steadfastly will, with regard to the manifestation of the experiences and realizations of the respective four yogas described above, automatically journey through the progressive stages of the five paths and ten bhumis of the general vehicles in their entirety. The *King of Samadhi Sutra* says:

> The person who adheres to this supreme samadhi
> And who upholds its teaching will, wherever he
> goes,
> Have gentle behavior and be utterly at peace.
> The joyous, the stainless, and the radiant,
> The brilliant, the hard to conquer, and the realized
> bhumi,
> The reaching far, the unshakable, and the good
> intelligence,
> The cloud of dharma—thus he will attain the ten
> bhumis.

THE FIVE PATHS

In other words, on the lesser, medium, and higher stages of the path of accumulation you achieve the four applications of mindfulness, the four right exertions, and the four legs of miraculous action. They all are complete within this swift path of mahamudra in the following way:

First of all, the general preliminaries are the reflection on the sufferings of samsara, the difficult to find freedoms and riches, the impermanence of life, and so forth. These aspects completely contain the four applications of mindfulness: mindfulness of the body as impure, mindfulness of sensations as painful, mindfulness of mind as impermanent, and mindfulness of phenomena as devoid of self-entity. Concentrating on the key points of these preliminaries and gaining some experience or certainty in them is therefore called traversing the lesser path of accumulation.

Similarly, the four right exertions of not producing unvirtuous qualities, abandoning those that have arisen, developing virtuous qualities, and increasing the ones that have arisen are in this context all included within taking refuge, arousing bodhichitta, the hundred syllables, and the mandala offerings, which therefore are called traversing the medium path of accumulation.

Following that, guru yoga includes the four legs of miraculous action: engendering one-pointed devotion to the guru is the miraculous leg of determination. Receiving the four empowerments is the leg of discernment. Supplicating is the leg of diligence. And finally mingling the guru and one's own mind together is the miraculous leg of concentration. Through them you traverse the greater path of accumulation.

The paramita vehicle teaches that the qualities of having perfected the path of accumulation are that you can journey to pure realms and meet the nirmanakaya buddhas in person and so forth. In this context, the eminent master is the essence of all the three kayas of buddhahood and his field of conversion is no other than a nirmanakaya realm; this, therefore, is in harmony with the above meaning.

The lesser, medium, and higher stages at the time of one-pointedness are the path of joining, which includes the four aspects of ascertainment: Seeing the essence of mind is called heat; gaining certainty therein is called summit; being unharmed by circumstances is acceptance; and being uninterrupted in one-pointed practice is called the supreme mundane quality of the path of joining.

At this time you also gain the specific qualities of the

five faculties: Gaining boundless certainty is the faculty of faith. Looking into the nature undistractedly is the faculty of mindfulness. Not being interrupted by laziness is the faculty of diligence. Being uninterrupted in meditation is the faculty of concentration. Realizing the definitive meaning is the faculty of discriminating knowledge. These five faculties having become individually perfected or turned into a strength are also called the five strengths.

Having in this way realized the three stages of one-pointedness, you have perfected the path of joining and arrived at simplicity. Because of seeing the truth of a realization which was not seen earlier, you have attained the path of seeing.

The paramita vehicle teaches that at this point one cultivates the seven bodhi-factors; in this context they are automatically present. In other words, abiding in the state of dharmata, the natural state as it is, is the bodhi-factor of samadhi. Not to be mixed with disturbing emotions is the bodhi-factor of fully discerning phenomena. Since the defilements to be relinquished through the path of seeing are naturally purified simply by remembering this samadhi, this is the bodhi-factor of mindfulness. Being freed from laziness and distraction, this is the bodhi-factor of diligence. Since you enjoy unconditioned bliss, this is the bodhi-factor of joy. Since all objects to be relinquished are purified, this is the bodhi-factor of pliancy. Because of realizing samsara and nirvana to be equality, this is the bodhi-factor of impartiality. Thus are the seven bodhi-factors perfected.

It is further taught that you attain the numerous qualities of the path of seeing as well as infinite samadhi doors.

Some masters hold that the path of cultivation and the first bhumi have been attained at the moment of perfecting the three stages of simplicity and arriving at one taste.

Most other masters accept that the attainment of the first bhumi is exactly the postmeditation after having seen the essence of simplicity and given rise to the path of seeing. The different levels of individual capacity obviously make fixed generalizations impossible. It is thus unquestionable that there are various types of scope and speed in traversing the paths.

The genuine realization of the path of seeing arising in this way is called "bhumi" since it is the source of or forms the basis for all good qualities. The *Avatamsaka Sutra* teaches:

> As soon as the bhumi is attained you are free from
>   five fears:
> Free from the fear of harm, of death, or of falling
>   into the lower realms,
> Free from the fear of being in samsara, and free
>   from anxiety.

In this way, the qualities of the ten bhumis increase further and further.

The period following the attainment of the bhumi is called the path of cultivation. Why is that? The path of cultivation is so called because you accustom yourself to the nature of the path of seeing.

At this point, you engage in the eightfold noble path. On this path of cultivation, in the meditation state you cultivate exclusively an unconditioned samadhi and, in the ensuing experience, the eight aspects of the noble path, which are regarded as conditioned. What are these eight? They are right view, thought, speech, conduct, livelihood, effort, mindfulness, and right concentration. In short, being nothing but accomplishments of a perfect nature, they are fully endowed with numerous qualities, which are especially exalted above the steps of the path below.

THE TEN BHUMIS

The first of the ten bhumis is called the joyous because of taking great delight in the special qualities. By means of the meditation state, which is nonconceptual nonarising, and the postmeditation state, which is illusory, you traverse the path chiefly through practicing the paramita of generosity with a frame of mind free from dread or faintheartedness even when sacrificing your head or limbs and so forth for the sake of sentient beings. In this way the general vehicle indeed has extensive details teaching the ten paramitas combined with the ten bhumis in progressive order. In this context they are as follows.

Since at the first stage of simplicity the joy of samadhi is greatly increased, you reach the first bhumi of the joyful. Being free from the defilements of what is to be relinquished through the path of cultivation, you reach the second bhumi of the stainless. Accomplishing the welfare of beings through the power of realization, you reach the third bhumi of the radiant.

At the medium stage of simplicity, the supreme buddha qualities being further increased, you reach the fourth bhumi of the brilliant. Because of purifying all the defilements of the tendencies that are difficult to purify through having realized emptiness and compassion as a unity, you reach the fifth bhumi of the hard to conquer.

At the time of realizing the greater simplicity, due to realizing samsara and nirvana to be nonarising, you reach the sixth bhumi of the realized. The bhumis up to this point are taught as being common to those of the shravakas and pratyekabuddhas.

Following this, dualistic experiences such as meditation and postmeditation, samsara and nirvana, are for the most part liberated as a unity, and thus the beginning of this realization of one taste is the seventh bhumi of reaching far.

Unmoved from the correct mindfulness of what is to be realized, you are at the medium one taste, the eighth bhumi of the unshakable. When the remaining defilements except for the very subtle, such as the illusory dualistic experience, are purified, you are at the higher stage of one taste, the ninth bhumi of good intelligence.

When this subtle dualistic experience is also naturally purified, all the qualities of the paths and bhumis have been perfected. There still remains, however, the obscuration of dualistic knowledge, which is the habitual tendency for fixation, an extremely subtle defilement of the remainder of the all-ground consciousness. It is, in this context, the time of the lesser and medium stages of nonmeditation, which according to the general system is called the tenth bhumi of the cloud of dharma. Up to this point, you possess qualities equal in status to the bodhisattva lords of the ten bhumis.

BUDDHAHOOD

The defilement of not knowing the nonconceptual nature, the subtle tendency for dualistic knowledge, then also dissolves into great self-existing self-cognizance, the essence of vajralike wisdom, and you are permanently free from all obscurations. The power of the wisdom of the nature as it is and of all that exists, as well as the strength of knowledge, compassion, and capacity are fully perfected. The outer and general vehicles describe this point as the supreme path of completion, the actual state of perfect buddhahood which here, in the context of mahamudra, is called the greater nonmeditation.

According to the general secret mantra, you are now free from the obscurations of karma, disturbing emotions, and habitual tendencies and have therefore no more path to train in, traverse, or realize. But in terms of the particular degree of increase in qualities, there is the eleventh bhumi of the universal light and the twelfth bhumi of the lotus of nonattachment. Having from one moment to the next realized these two extraordinary inner bhumis, the rupakayas for the benefit of others as the expression of having perfected dharmakaya for the benefit of yourself, you then continuously accomplish the great welfare of beings throughout space for as long as samsara has not been emptied. That is called the thirteenth bhumi of the vajra holder, buddhahood itself.

As long as these paths and bhumis have something higher to journey toward, they are called the path of learning. Reaching the ultimate, where there is no higher place to travel to, is called the path of nonlearning. Thus the thirteenth bhumi of the vajra holder is the final fruition of the inner secret mantra.

THE QUALITIES

What special qualities accompany the attainment of these bhumis? Attaining the first bhumi you can journey simultaneously to one hundred nirmanakaya realms in the ten directions, see one hundred buddhas in person, and hear the dharma. You can simultaneously perform one hundred different acts of generosity, such as sacrificing even life and limb, kingdom, children, and wife without second thoughts. You can simultaneously emanate one hundred different rays of light, radiating red light while absorbing white light, sending forth yellow light while being encircled in blue light, emanating many while reabsorbing a few, and so forth. You can simultaneously teach one-hundred dharma-doors, each in conformity with the individual dispositions, capacities, and inclinations of one hundred different disciples. You can simultaneously enter one hundred different samadhis, such as the courageous movement, the subjugating, and the majestic lion, which have been taught in the Prajnaparamita by the Victorious One. You can simultaneously show one hundred different kinds of miraculous displays, such as flying through the sky or moving through the earth, going unimpededly through mountains or rocks, and not sinking down into water. You can also send forth flames from the upper part of the body and water from the lower or vice versa, as well as creating apparitions and transformations of letting one appear as many forms or absorbing many into one. These are the seven times one hundred qualities over which you gain mastery.

Likewise, in progression, you will on the second bhumi have seven times one thousand of these qualities, on the third seven times ten thousand, on the fourth seven times one hundred thousand, on the fifth seven times one million, on the sixth seven times ten million, on the seventh seven times one hundred million, on the eighth seven times one billion, on the ninth seven times ten billion, on the tenth seven times one hundred billion, on the eleventh seven times one trillion, and on the twelfth seven times ten trillion. On realizing the thirteenth bhumi of the vajra holder, the nature of the three kayas of buddhahood, the number of supreme qualities is infinite. This nature transcends the limits of conceptual thinking and can be measured by no one.

HOW THE QUALITIES MANIFEST

This path of mahamudra, the pinnacle of the vehicles, contains the ten bhumis and five paths taught in the general vehicles in their entirety and without being mixed together. The nature of things, therefore, is that a person who correctly realizes the four yogas will gradually or instantaneously perfect all the qualities of these paths and bhumis. For some people these qualities are, however, not superficially present to be perceived as something concretely visible. That is the nature of the hidden short path of the secret mantra. Most birds and wild animals after being born from their mother's womb must yet develop their bodily strength to gradually become equal to their mother. The garuda bird, ruler of the feathered race, or on the other hand the lion, king of the wild animals, perfects its strength within the egg or the womb where it is indeed not perceived by others. Once born, by the power of having fully perfected its strength, it is immediately able to act on its own, such as flying together with its mother through the skies.

Similarly, the signs of realization do not visibly manifest as long as the practitioner remains encased within his material body; later, however, with the disintegration of the bodily encasement and the ripening of fruition, perfection of the qualities will occur simultaneously.

Nonetheless, many people, concentrating on the key points of the path of united means and knowledge, visibly manifest within their very bodies the signs of the path, such as the miracles and superknowledges. But in actuality, without having attained mastery over the sameness of space and wisdom, the mind beyond conceptual thinking, the natural state of the essence of things, and the true innate wisdom, some so-called siddhas are possessed by the demon of arrogance and become overjoyed by, cling to as excellent, and regard as supreme the mere fragments of signs of attainment in the practices of development and completion, of the nadis, pranas, and bindus, and so forth. They only herd themselves and others into the lower realms. They are abundant nowadays; so beware, all intelligent people!

ENHANCEMENT

Having in this way briefly described the view and meditation, the paths and the bhumis, I shall also explain in short how to practice the conduct, the application of enhancement.

According to most paths of secret mantra, the different types of conduct mentioned are the three of elaborate, unelaborate, and very unelaborate conduct. There are also secret conduct, group conduct, awareness discipline, the completely victorious conduct, and so forth. Many such categories exist, but they are for the most part general enhancements for the stages of development and completion. In this context, the ever-excellent conduct, sustaining the natural mode of the innate, free from conceptual mind, is alone important.

First of all, even during the preliminary stages of gathering the accumulations, purifying the obscurations, and the means for receiving the blessings, you should exert yourself in practicing the ever-excellent conduct of being untainted by the defilement of any of the eight worldly concerns and of not feeling ashamed of yourself.

Next, when gaining certainty about the view and meditation of the main part of practice and becoming clear about self-cognizance, you should exert yourself in the ever-excellent conduct of being skilled in all by knowing one and knowing one that liberates all. That is the means of hammering down the nails of many plans from within yourself and cutting through the arrogance of doubt in your own mind.

Finally, although various authoritative scriptures and oral instructions have taught different types of conduct as means to enhance one's practice, the essential key points are as follows: Cut your worldly attachments completely and live companionless in secluded mountain retreats; that is the conduct of a wounded deer. Be free from fear or anxiety in the face of difficulties; that is the conduct of a lion sporting in the mountains. Be free from attachment or clinging to sense pleasures; that is the conduct of the wind in the sky. Do not become involved in the fetters of accepting or rejecting the eight worldly concerns; that is the conduct of a madman. Sustain simply and unrestrictedly the natural flow of your mind while unbound by the ties of dualistic fixation; that is the conduct of a spear stabbing in space.

While engaging in these types of conduct, cut the fetters of deluded wandering, distraction, hope and fear. Becoming involved in even as much as a hair tip of the inner fault of desiring to have signs and indications, experience and realization, or siddhis, and so forth will gain you nothing but obscuring your real condition, your innate state, the natural face of dharmakaya. Focus exclusively on sustaining the unconstructed innate nature; that is the most eminent ever-excellent conduct of bringing things into the path.

Regardless of what various difficulties such as conceptual thinking, disturbing emotions, suffering, fear, sickness, or death temporarily occur, be able to bring these into the path as the main part of the natural mahamudra practice, neither hoping for nor relying on some other means of benefit through an antidote. That is the king of all types of enhancement.

The person able to practice like this will gain mastery over all of samsara and nirvana, appearance and existence.

Enhancement

So, the nature of things is that you will be free from any basis of obstacles, the great ocean of siddhis will overflow, the darkness of the two obscurations will be cleared, the sun of signs and accomplishment will shine forth, the buddha will be discovered within your own mind, and the treasury of benefiting others will be opened wide.

It is, on the contrary, indeed cause for despair to see the meditators who seem to be exclusively throwing away the single sufficient jewel that has been placed in their hands, and like a child picking flowers they spend a lifetime wishing for one better thing to do after another.

SECTION THREE

FRUITION MAHAMUDRA

THE THREE KAYAS
OF BUDDHAHOOD

Having briefly described the nature of the ground and the path, the view, meditation, and conduct, I shall now conclude with the third major point: explaining the meaning of fruition mahamudra, the inseparability of the three kayas or the unity of the two kayas.

DHARMAKAYA

When a gifted practitioner has seen the natural face of ground mahamudra, the innate state, and focusing on the key points of practicing path mahamudra, the view and meditation, has reached perfection in the training, he has at this point realized the final fruition mahamudra, the ultimate dharmakaya.

The essence of dharmakaya is self-cognizant and unfabricated original wakefulness,* unchanging and free from increase or decrease, primordially present in the mind-stream of all sentient beings of the three realms. This is exactly what is to be realized through the means of practice, the profound key points of the path. Besides this wakefulness there is nothing other, no new or unprecedented buddha or dharmakaya that is to appear. The characteristics of dharmakaya are as follows.

Being endowed with the wisdom of knowing the nature as it is and with the wisdom of all existent objects of knowledge, it is called endowed with the twofold knowl-

---

*Tib. ye shes, usually and otherwise translated as "wisdom."

edge. Since the essence is primordially and utterly pure and since the passing, coemergent defilements are purified, dharmakaya is also said to be endowed with the twofold purity. Actually, it is free from the defilement of not knowing or not perceiving all knowable phenomena and has fully perfected all aspects of good qualities.

The dharmakaya's unobstructed expression of manifestation, the display of this wakefulness, gives rise to the two kayas of sambhogakaya and nirmanakaya.

SEVEN ASPECTS OF UNITY

These three kayas possess the qualities of being endowed with the seven aspects of unity. What are these seven?

(1) The aspect of enjoyment is due to perpetually and continually utilizing the dharma-wheels of the profound, the extensive, and the secret mantra for all the great bodhisattvas in the abode of Akanishtha. (2) The aspect of union is due to the wisdom body of perfect marks and signs being united with the consort of its natural radiance. (3) The aspect of great bliss is due to unconditioned great bliss being unceasing. These three are the special attributes of sambhogakaya.

(4) The aspect of being totally filled with compassion is nonconceptual compassion, all-encompassing, like space. (5) The aspect of continuity is the occurrence, spontaneously and without concepts, of vast activity equal to the limits of samsara. (6) The aspect of uninterruptedness is not dwelling on the peaceful extreme of nirvana. These three are the special attributes of nirmanakaya.

(7) The aspect of absence of self-nature, since the unity of emptiness and compassion is totally free from mental constructs and thus devoid of a self-nature, is regarded as the special attribute of dharmakaya. In this way the three kayas are endowed with seven aspects.

The Three Kayas

EIGHT MASTERIES OF SAMBHOGAKAYA

It is also taught that the three kayas possess the eight qualities of mastery:

(1) Being endowed with all the aspects of taming whoever needs to be tamed in whichever way is necessary is the mastery of body. (2) The unceasing wheel of dharma to tame whomever is in need is the mastery of speech. (3) Possessing nonconceptual compassion is the mastery of mind. (4) Unimpeded miraculous powers are the mastery of miracles. (5) The true enlightenment of samsara and nirvana and the three times as being equal and of one taste is the mastery of all-pervasiveness. (6) Being untainted by desire even when presented with sense pleasures by offering goddesses equal in number to the dust motes of thirty-two Sumerus is the mastery of desire. (7) Fulfilling the desires and hopes of beings in accordance with their wishes as does a wish-fulfilling gem is the mastery of granting whatever is desired. (8) Abiding continually as the dharma king over the three realms in the dharmadhatu palace of Akanishtha is the mastery of abode. Possessing the eight masteries is one description of the qualities of sambhogakaya.

NIRMANAKAYA

The nirmanakayas are emanated as the inconceivable manifestation of dharmakaya and sambhogakaya. Thus emanated to tame beings, these reflections of the moon correspond to the number of vessels of water where they appear. The appearance of infinite and numberless emanations to tame whomever is in need in whichever way is necessary, be it through the nirmanakayas of creation, of incarnation, or of great enlightenment and so forth, is known as the inexhaustible adornment wheel of the secrets of the body, speech, and mind of all the buddhas.

65

Fruition Mahamudra

THE CAUSES FOR ACCOMPLISHING THE KAYAS

The actual fruition of focusing on the key point of the ultimate emptiness of mahamudra right now at the time of the path is the accomplishment of dharmakaya. As the subsidiary part of that, the aspect of means, you will accomplish nirmanakaya purely through the power of developing bodhichitta, making aspirations, and so forth. You attain the sambhogakaya through the causation of having practiced the profound development stage. Thus through the power of endeavoring in these practices, not in a differentiated or sporadic way but as the unity of means and knowledge, the great and complete threefold purity, you will attain stability in the essence within which the three kayas are inseparable.

The three kayas explained here as well as the numerous classifications of four or five kayas are one identity with different names given to the various qualities or functions. They are in short nothing other than the present essence, nature, and expression of your mind which, at the time of fruition, are called the three kayas.

SUMMARY

In this context, the causal vehicles and the lower tantras of mantra contain numberless commentaries and systems adhering to particular points of view as well as quotations intended for another purpose or with a concealed intent: whether or not dharmakaya has a face and arms; whether its realm is demonstrable or not demonstrable; whether or not a buddha has wisdom comprised of his own stream-of-being; and whether or not the two rupakayas have sensation as personal experience and so forth. These many subjects of debate along with their proofs and refutations indeed seem complicated. But while these topics are all surely valid, each in its own context, here, in the quintessence of vehicles, one need not depend upon establishing the views of the lower vehicles.

The meaning here is known as "in harmony with all yet exalted above them." What does this meaning intend? Do not apprehend, do not cling to, do not refute, and do not establish any of all the phenomena comprising samsara and nirvana, appearance and existence, as being either real or unreal, existent or nonexistent, true or untrue, arising or ceasing, coming or going, permanent or annihilated. One who holds them to be nonexistent falls into the extreme of nihilism, and one who holds them to be existent falls into the extreme of eternalism. Thinking, "They are neither existent nor nonexistent" also does not transcend mental fabrication. So if something exists in the experience of others, then let it exist because unobstructed perception is inexhaustible, and the coincidence of causation is unfailing. If something is nonexistent in the perception of others, then let it be nonexistent since in essence it has never moved away from emptiness, the nature of possessing no existence whatsoever. If something is held to be neither existent nor nonexistent, then let that also be true as it falls into neither extreme and is also not confined to any category of classification.

All things appearing as the external world and beings are perceived by impure sentient beings' deluded habitual tendencies and karmic experiences as the material and solid five elements. Practitioners on the path perceive all things as the unceasing display of their own minds. The buddhas and bodhisattvas perceive things as the realms of self-manifest wakefulness. Ultimately, everything is no more than the magical display of the mind-essence.

Similarly, all the inner cognitive acts and thoughts of the mental states are, for impure deluded beings, of the nature of karma, disturbing emotions, and habitual tendencies. For practitioners on the path, cognitive acts are the different aspects of the view and meditation, experience and realization. Finally, for the sugata buddhas of the three kayas, cognitive acts are the wisdom display of knowledge and loving kindness.

Although not even an atom of difference exists in the natural state of the ground, the difference lies in whether it is totally enveloped in the passing conceptual obscurations (as in the case of all sentient beings), whether it is slightly covered (as in the case of practitioners on the path), or whether it is free from obscurations (as in the case of the buddhas).*

The key point of sole importance is therefore to relax into the state of mahamudra, your own unfabricated mind, the essential nature that has never been transcended (since the primordial beginning), is not transcending (in the present), and will never transcend (in the future) the essence of ground, path, and fruition, the union of the two kayas, or the indivisibility of the three kayas.

Those who form exaggerations and denigrations about the unconditioned nature with their conditioned intellects, who cling to the limitations of words and argue while adhering to partisan philosophical schools are childish, trying to grasp the extent of the sky. Rest therefore in great, all-pervasive equality in the expanse of unconstructed naturalness. There is then no doubt that, beyond the concepts of journey and traveler, you will be liberated into the nature endowed with the spontaneously present fruition of the four yogas, the ten bhumis, the five paths, and the three kayas.

---

*The original manuscript contains these parenthetical remarks as footnotes.

EPILOGUE

KYEHO!
The nature of sugata-essence, originally free since the
   beginning,
The buddhahood of the spontaneously present three kayas,
Is in all beings down to the tiniest insect,
Always present without separation though obscured by
   ignorance.

Though dharma-doors equal in number to those to be
   tamed are taught to tame beings,
They remain deluded by their impure personal perceptions,
On mistaken paths,[1] wrong paths,[2] errant paths,[3] and
   fettered by their paths;[4]
To journey on the excellent and perfect path is as rare as
   the udumbara flower.

Chained in fixation on extremes while transcending extremes (the view),
Not recognized, like the treasure of a destitute, while
   present in oneself (the meditation),
Spoiled by fabrication while self-manifesting and unfabricated (the action)—
What a great blunder not recognizing the nature of things
   as they are!

---

[1] All worldly people.
[2] All the non-Buddhists.
[3] The followers of hinayana.
[4] The followers of the lower tantras. (This and the preceding three
footnotes are found in the original manuscript.)

Epilogue

The strong and wealthy become possessed by their merit.[5]
People bloated with learning become hardened, like but-
   ter-skin.[6]
Ignorant meditators persevere in rigidity, as if trying to
   press oil from sand;[7]
Who then is endowed with mahamudra of the natural
   state?

Kyihu!
The supreme teaching of sutra and tantra, like the pair of
   the sun and the moon,
Is now only partly present,
Like the vermilion glow on clouds after the sunset in the
   west;
What is the point in casting freedoms and riches in the
   gutter for this life's sake?

Living in unpeopled mountain hermitages,
Relying merely on simple food to support one's life
While looking into the innate natural face, the eminent
   permanent goal—
Is this not the tradition of the Practice Lineage?

Nowadays deeds claimed to benefit the teachings cause its
   degeneration,
And endeavor is not for attaining the genuine truth;
Who will need and who will appreciate
These sporadic writings by someone like me?

I may fill my room with pages of scribbles
Not needed by myself and not appreciated by others.

---

[5]They lack the fortune to practice meditation.
[6]A traditional example for being jaded and insensitive; a cow hide
containing the butter becomes rigid instead of being cured and becoming pliable.
[7]They do not comprehend the key points of meditation practice. (These
three footnotes are found in the original manuscript.)

Epilogue

Incapable of taming the mind of even one person,
They are naught but paper, ink, and tiring labor for my
  fingers.

Unable to refuse the request
Of someone who for a long time has insistently pleaded,
I have uttered this simply from presumptuousness,
While it lacks any power of a flawless composition of
  words with consistent meaning.

Lacking discernment that masters the expressing word
As well as experience of having realized the great expressed
  meaning,
How can this composition
Possibly become anything more than a laughing stock for
  learned and accomplished beings?

Nevertheless, this beautiful garland of blossoming white
  lotuses,
Illuminated by a noble motivation and unobscured by evil
  intent,
May just possibly become an ornament for the ears
Of some simple aspirant meditators like myself.

By the merit of having written this,
Combined with all conditioned and unconditioned virtue
  of samsara, nirvana, and the path,
May the Practice Lineage teachings flourish throughout all
  directions,
And may all beings realize the fruition of mahamudra.

  For a long time I was repeatedly requested by Tsultrim
Sangpo, the vidyadhara of Mangom, in these words:
"Please write a detailed and extensive textbook of necessary instructions on enhancement and the signs of the
stages of the path for practitioners of the mahamudra of

definitive meaning." But as an endless number of these types of books, both profound and extensive, exist in the collected works of the forefathers of the Practice Lineage, there was no need to compose another.

However, I have indeed been considered with affection by many kind refuge masters and have received the following works on the profound path of mahamudra:

Uniting with the Coemergent,[8] the *Four Words*,[9] *Gangama*,[10] the *Letterless*,[11] the teachings on the *Root of Symbols*[12] and the *Essence of Accomplishment*,[13] the *Inconceivable Secret*,[14] the *Illuminating Wisdom*,[15] the *Fivefold*,[16] the *Wish-Fulfilling Jewel*,[17] the *Six Nails of Key Points*,[18] as well as numerous other teachings of direct instructions famed among the New Schools. From the Old School teaching, I have kindly been given the *Limitless Expanse of Mahamudra*,[19] the *Circle of the Sun*,[20] the *Single Arisen Awareness*,[21] *Dispelling the Darkness of Ignorance*,[22] *Directly Seeing the Innate*,[23] as well as numerous other works of revealed termas.

---

[8]Tib. lhan cig skyes sbyor, by Gampopa.
[9]Tib. yi ge bzhi pa, by Maitripa.
[10]Tib. gang ga ma. A song of mahamudra by Tilopa. A translation of this precious teaching by Chögyam Trungpa Rinpoche is found in *The Myth of Freedom* (Shambhala Publications, 1976).
[11]Tib. yi ge med pa.
[12]Tib. brda rtsa, by Maitripa.
[13]Tib. grub snying.
[14]Tib. gsang ba bsam gyis mi khyab pa, a tantra.
[15]Tib. ye shes gsal byed, by Milarepa.
[16]Tib. lnga ldan, by Drigung Kyobpa Sumgön.
[17]Tib. yid bzhin nor bu.
[18]Tib. gnad kyi gzer drug, by Tilopa.
[19]Tib. phyag chen klong yangs mtha' bral.
[20]Tib. nyi ma'i snying po.
[21]Tib. rig pa gcig skyes.
[22]Tib. ma rig mun sel, by the ninth Karmapa.
[23]Tib. gnyug ma gcer mthong. According to Tulku Urgyen Rinpoche, this text is probably the rig pa gcer mthong from the cycle of Karling

Epilogue

Despite receiving all these teachings, I possess no ability or courage to compose such a work. Having been tossed about on the waves of karma, disturbing emotions, and distraction, consequently not even the tiniest fraction of experience or realization of their meaning has arisen within my mind.

However, I beg wholeheartedly that all intelligent people will not despise these writings made by a blind man in a dense darkness simply in order not to turn down the word of the one who asked me.

By the virtue of this may all beings throughout space, my past mothers, attain within this very lifetime the sublime state of unexcelled enlightenment.

> May it be virtuous!
> May it be virtuous!
> May it be virtuous!

Shitro (kar gling zhi khro), a translation of which is in *The Tibetan Book of the Great Liberation,* edited by Evans-Wentz (Oxford University Press, 1954).

TRANSLATOR'S AFTERWORD

In accordance with the command of His Holiness Dilgo Khyentse Rinpoche and the kind encouragement and teachings of Tulku Urgyen Rinpoche and Chökyi Nyima Rinpoche, this inadequate rendering was made by Erik Pema Kunsang at Nagi Gompa, 1987. May it be a cause for many practitioners to realize mahamudra.

GLOSSARY

This glossary was compiled partly from questions to Tulku Chökyi Nyima Rinpoche and Tulku Urgyen Rinpoche, to give general readers a rough idea about the different uncommon expressions used in the translation. The translator has tried to refrain from personal interpretations and kept strictly to what he has heard from his teachers. This glossary does not attempt to give exhaustive explanations. The Tibetan equivalents have been included so that one can have the more profound terms clarified by Tibetan-speaking masters. Many of the English terms were coined exclusively for use in this translation and may have been phrased differently in another context.

ACCEPTANCE (bzod pa) One of the four aspects of ascertainment on the path of joining.

ACCUMULATIONS *See* Two accumulations.

ACHARYA SHANTIPA (slob dpon shan ti pa) An Indian master in the mahamudra lineage.

AGGREGATE (phung po) *See* Five skandhas.

AKANISHTHA ('og min) The "highest"; the realm of Vajradhara, the dharmakaya buddha. For a discussion of the various types of Akanishtha, see Gyurme Dorje's forthcoming translation of Longchen Rabjam's *Phyogs bCu Mun Sel*.

ALAYA (kun gzhi) The basis of all of samsara and nirvana. *See also* All-ground.

ALL-ENCOMPASSING PURITY (dag pa rab 'byams) The skandhas, elements, and so forth of the world and beings are, in their pure aspects, the five male and female buddhas.

ALL-GROUND (kun gzhi, alaya) The basis of mind and both pure and impure phenomena. This word has different mean-

Glossary

ings in different contexts and should be understood accordingly. Literally it means the "foundation of all things."

ALL-GROUND CONSCIOUSNESS (kun gzhi'i rnam par shes pa) The cognizant aspect of the all-ground, like the brightness of a mirror.

ALL-GROUND OF VARIOUS TENDENCIES (bag chags sna tshogs pa'i kun gzhi) The alaya serving as the basis for samsaric tendencies.

APPEARANCE AND EXISTENCE (snang srid) Whatever can be experienced (the five elements) and has a possibility of existence (the five aggregates). This term usually refers to the world and sentient beings.

ATTRIBUTE (mtshan ma).

AUTHORITATIVE SCRIPTURES (gzhung) Books on philosophy with established validity.

Avatamsaka Sutra (mdo phal po che) A sutra belonging to the third turning of the wheel of dharma. Translated into English and published as *The Flower Adornment Scripture,* vols. 1–3, translated by Thomas Cleary (Shambhala Publications, 1984–87).

AVICHI HELL (mnar med kyi dmyal ba) The lowest of the eight hot hells.

AWARENESS DISCIPLINE (rig pa rtul zhugs) Action free from accepting and rejecting.

BASIC STRAYING FROM THE ESSENCE OF EMPTINESS (stong nyid gshis shor)

BASIC STRAYING FROM THE PATH (lam gyi gshis shor)

BASIC STRAYING FROM THE REMEDY (gnyen po gshis shor)

BASIC STRAYING INTO GENERALIZED EMPTINESS (stong nyid rgyas 'debs su gshis shor)

BHUMI (sa) *See* Ten bhumis.

BINDU (thig le) *See* Nadi, prana, and bindu.

BODHICHITTA (byang sems, byang chub kyi sems) The aspiration to attain enlightenment for the sake of all beings.

BRAHMIN (bram ze) A person belonging to the priestly caste.

78

Glossary

BRILLIANT ('od 'phro ba) The fourth of the ten bodhisattva bhumis.

BUDDHA OF YOUR OWN MIND (rang sems sangs rgyas) The enlightened essence of one's own mind.

BUDDHAHOOD (sangs rgyas) The perfect and complete enlightenment of dwelling in neither samsara nor nirvana.

CAUSAL VEHICLES (rgyu'i theg pa) Same as the two vehicles, hinayana and mahayana. The practitioners of these vehicles regard the practices as the cause for attaining fruition.

CHITTAMATRA (sems tsam pa) The Mind-Only school of mahayana, asserting the view that all phenomena are "only" the appearances of "mind."

CHÖ (gcod) Literally "cutting." A system of practices based on prajnaparamita and set down by Machik Labdrön for the purpose of cutting through the four maras and ego-clinging. One of the Eight Practice Lineages of Buddhism in Tibet.

CHÖKYI NYIMA RINPOCHE (chos kyi nyi ma rin po che) The abbot of Ka-Nying Shedrup Ling Monastery and the oldest son of Tulku Urgyen Rinpoche. Author of *Union of Mahamudra and Dzogchen* and *Jewel of the Heart* (Rangjung Yeshe Publications, 1986 and 1987).

CLOUD OF DHARMA (chos kyi sprin) The tenth of the ten bodhisattva levels.

COEMERGENT (lhan cig skyes pa) The two aspects of mind, appearance and emptiness, coexist. As is said: "Coemergent mind is dharmakaya; coemergent appearance is the light of dharmakaya."

COEMERGENT IGNORANCE (lhan cig skyes pa'i ma rig pa) "Coemergent" means arising together with or coexisting with one's mind, like sandalwood and its fragrance. "Ignorance" here means lack of knowledge of the nature of mind. In mahamudra practice this is the deluded aspect, the moment of oblivion that allows confused thinking to occur.

COEMERGENT WISDOM (lhan cig skyes pa'i ye shes) The innate wakefulness potentially present in all sentient beings. "Wisdom" here means the "primordially undeluded wakefulness."

COGNIZANT QUALITY (gsal cha)   The mind's inherent capacity for knowing.

COMMON VEHICLES (thun mong gi theg pa)   A term for hinayana and mahayana taken together and compared with the "supreme vehicle," vajrayana.

COMPLETE ENLIGHTENMENT (rdzogs pa'i byang chub) Synonymous with *buddhahood.*

COMPLETION STAGE (rdzogs rim)   "Completion stage with marks" is the six doctrines of Naropa. "Completion stage without marks" is the practice of essence mahamudra. *See also* Development and completion.

CONCEPT AND DISCERNMENT (rtog dpyod)   Gross conception and fine discrimination.

CONCEPTUAL IGNORANCE (kun tu brtags pa'i ma rig pa)   In vajrayana, the ignorance of conceptualizing subject and object. In the sutra system, superimposed or learned wrong views. Specifically, in mahamudra practice it means conceptual thinking.

CONFUSION AND LIBERATION ('khrul grol)   Synonymous with *samsara and nirvana.*

CONSCIOUSNESSES OF THE FIVE SENSES (sgo lnga'i rnam par shes pa)   The acts of cognizing visual form, sound, smell, taste, and texture.

CUTTING THROUGH (khregs chod)   Cutting through the stream of the thoughts of the three times. *See also* Trekchö.

DAKPO KAGYU (dvags po bka' brgyud)   The Kagyu lineage as transmitted through Gampopa, who is also known as Dakpo Lhaje, the "Doctor from Dakpo."

DEFILED MIND (nyon yid, nyon mongs pa'i yid kyi rnam par shes pa)   The aspect of mind which, taking the all-ground as reference, conceives the thought "I am"; one of the eight collections of consciousnesses.

DEFINITIVE MEANING (nges pa'i don)   The direct teachings on emptiness and luminosity as opposed to the "expedient meaning" (drang don), which leads to the definitive meaning.

Glossary

DEPENDENT (gzhan dbang)   *See* Three natures.

DEPENDENT ORIGINATION (rten cing 'brel bar 'byung ba)   The natural law that all phenomena arise "dependent upon" their own causes "in connection with" their individual conditions. The fact that no phenomena appear without a cause and none are made by an uncaused creator, but all arise exclusively due to the coincidence of causes and conditions.

DESIRE, FORM, AND FORMLESSNESS, THE REALMS OF ('dod gzugs gzugs med kyi khams)   The three realms of samsaric existence.

DESIRE REALM ('dod khams)   Comprised of the abodes of hell beings, hungry ghosts, animals, humans, asuras, and the gods of the six abodes of desire; it is called "desire realm" because of the torment by mental pain caused by gross desire and attachment. One of the "three realms."

DEVELOPMENT AND COMPLETION (bskyed rdzogs)   The two main aspects of vajrayana practice. Development stage is fabricated by mind. Completion stage means resting in the unfabricated nature of mind. *See also* Completion; Development stage.

DEVELOPMENT STAGE (bskyed rim, utpattikrama)   One of the two aspects of vajrayana practice that is to create pure images mentally in order to purify habitual tendencies. *See also* Development and completion.

DHARMA (chos)   The Buddha's teachings; sometimes *dharma* can mean phenomena or mental objects as well as attributes or qualities.

DHARMA-DOORS (chos kyi sgo)   Figurative expression for the teachings of the buddhas.

DHARMA SECTIONS (chos kyi phung po)   Entities of different teachings such as the eighty-four thousand sections of the Buddha's words.

DHARMADHATU (chos kyi dbyings)   The "realm of phenomena"; the suchness in which emptiness and dependent origination are inseparable. In this context "dharma" means the truth and "dhatu" means space free from center or periphery. Another explanation is "the nature of phenomena" beyond arising, dwelling, and ceasing.

DHARMADHATU PALACE OF AKANISHTHA ('og min chos kyi

dbyings kyi pho brang) Figurative expression for the abode of Vajradhara, the dharmakaya buddha.

DHARMAKAYA (chos sku) The first of the three kayas, which is devoid of constructs, like space. The nature of all phenomena designated as "body." Should be understood individually according to ground, path, and fruition. *See also* Three kayas.

DHARMAKAYA OF SELF-COGNIZANCE (rang rig chos sku) The dharmakaya aspect of one's own mind.

DHARMAKAYA THRONE OF NONMEDITATION (bsgom med chos sku'i rgyal sa) The last stage in the yoga of nonmeditation, which is the complete collapse of fixation and conceptual mind, like a cloud free from the clouds of intellectual meditation. Synonymous with *complete enlightenment*.

DHARMATA (chos nyid) The nature of phenomena and mind.

DHYANA (bsam gtan) The state of concentrated mind with fixation, and also the god realms produced through such mental concentration.

DISTURBING EMOTIONS (nyon mongs pa) The five poisons of desire, anger, delusion, pride, and envy which tire, disturb, and torment one's mind.

Doha Kosha (do ha mdzod) A collection of spontaneous vajra songs by the Indian masters of the mahamudra lineage.

DRUKPA KAGYU SCHOOL ('brug pa bka' brgyud) The Kagyu teachings transmitted from Gampopa to Phagmo Drubpa, and from him to Lingje Repa.

DUALISTIC PHENOMENA (gnyis snang) Experience structured as perceiver and object perceived.

DZOGCHEN (rdzogs pa chen po; rdzogs chen) The teachings beyond the vehicles of causation, first taught in the human world by the great vidyadhara Garab Dorje. *See also* Mahasandhi.

DZOGCHEN OF THE NATURAL STATE (gnas lugs rdzogs pa chen po) Synonymous with *trekcho*, the view of *cutting through* and identical to *essence mahamudra*. See also the aforementioned terms.

EIGHT COLLECTIONS OF CONSCIOUSNESSES (rnam shes tshogs

Glossary

brgyad) The all-ground consciousness, mind-conscious-ness, defiled mind-consciousness, and the five sense-con-sciousnesses.

EIGHT DEVIATIONS (shor sa brgyad) The four basic and the four temporary strayings. *See also under* Basic straying and Tem-porary straying.

EIGHT PRACTICE LINEAGES (sgrub brgyud shing rta brgyad) The eight independent schools of Buddhism that flourished in Tibet; Nyingma, Kadampa, Marpa Kagyu, Shangpa Kagyu, Sakya, Jordruk, Shije, and Chö. *See also* Practice Lineage.

EIGHT QUALITIES OF MASTERY (dbang phyug brgyad)

EIGHT WORLDLY CONCERNS ('jig rten chos brgyad) Attachment to gain, pleasure, praise, and fame; and aversion to loss, pain, blame, and bad reputation.

EIGHTFOLD NOBLE PATH ('phags lam gyi yan lag brgyad) Literally the "eight aspects of the path of noble beings": right view, thought, speech, conduct, livelihood, effort, mindful-ness, concentration. These are perfected on the path of cultivation.

EIGHTY INHERENT THOUGHT STATES (rang bzhin brgyad cu'i rtog pa) Thirty-three resulting from anger, forty from desire, and seven from delusion. First, the thirty-three thought states resulting from anger, according to the *Spyod bsDus* composed by Aryadeva: detachment, medium detachment, intense de-tachment, inner mental going and coming, sadness, medium sadness, intense sadness, quietude, conceptualization, fear, medium fear, intense fear, craving, medium craving, intense craving, grasping, nonvirtue, mental pain due to hunger or thirst, sensation, medium sensation, intense sensation, cog-nizing, cognizance, perception-basis, discrimination, con-science, compassion, love, medium love, intense love, appre-hensiveness, attraction, and jealousy. Second, the forty thought states of desire, according to the *sPyod bsDus:* attach-ment, thorough lust, delight, medium delight, intense delight, rejoicing, strong joy, amazement, agitation, satisfac-tion, embracing, kissing, clasping, supporting, exertion, pride, engagement, infatuation, strength, joy, joining in bliss, medium joining in bliss, intense joining in bliss, gracefulness, strong flirtation, hostility, virtue, lucidity, truth, nontruth, ascertainment, grasping, generosity, encouragement, bravery, shamelessness, perkiness, viciousness, unrulyness, and strong deceitfulness. The seven thought states of delusion, according to the *sPyod bsDus:* medium desire, forgetfulness, confusion, speechlessness, weariness, laziness, and doubt.

EIGHTY MAHASIDDHAS (grub thob brgyad bcu, grub chen brgyad bcu)   Accomplished masters in the Indian lineages of vajrayana practice. For details of their life stories, see *Buddha's Lions* (Dharma Publishing) and *Masters of Mahamudra* (SUNY Press).

ELABORATE CONDUCT (spros bcas kyi spyod pa)   One of the various types of enhancement. Acts of procuring food and clothing, like a businessman, or keeping to detailed precepts and rituals.

EMANCIPATION GATE OF EMPTINESS (rnam par thar pa'i sgo stong pa nyid)   One of the "three gates of emancipation."

EMANCIPATION GATE OF MARKLESSNESS (rnam par thar pa'i sgo mtshan ma med pa)   One of the "three gates of emancipation."

EMANCIPATION GATE OF WISHLESSNESS (rnam par thar pa'i sgo smon pa med pa)   One of the "three gates of emancipation."

EMPOWERMENT (dbang)   The conferring of power or authorization to practice the vajrayana teachings, the indispensable entrance door to tantric practice.

ENSUING PERCEPTION (rjes snang)   The perceptions or appearances perceived during the postmeditation state.

ENSUING UNDERSTANDING (rjes shes)   The state of mind during the postmeditation state.

ESSENCE MAHAMUDRA (snying po'i phyag chen)   The essential view of mahamudra introduced directly and without being dependent upon philosophical reasoning (as in sutra mahamudra) or yogic practices (as in mantra mahamudra).

ESSENCE, NATURE, AND COMPASSION (ngo bo rang bzhin thugs rje)   The three aspects of the sugatagarbha according to the dzogchen system.

Glossary

ESSENCE, NATURE, AND EXPRESSION (gshis gdangs rtsal) The three aspects of the sugatagarbha according to the mahamudra system.

ESSENCE OF AWARENESS (rig ngo) Synonymous with the nature of mind.

ESSENTIAL NATURE OF THINGS (dngos po gshis kyi gnas lugs) *See* Suchness.

ETERNALISM (rtag lta) Belief in a permanent and causeless creator of everything. In particular, the belief that one's identity or consciousness has a concrete essence which is independent, everlasting, and singular.

EVER-EXCELLENT CONDUCT (kun tu bzang po'i spyod pa)

EXAGGERATION AND DENIGRATION (sgro btags + skur 'debs) Attaching existence or attributes to something that does not have them + underestimating the existence or attributes of something which does have them.

EXHAUSTION OF PHENOMENA BEYOND CONCEPTS (chos zad blo 'das) The fourth of the four visions of dzogchen. Synonymous with *complete enlightenment.*

EXPEDIENT MEANING (drang don) The teachings on conventional meaning designed to lead the practitioner to the "definitive meaning."

EXPERIENCE (nyams) Usually refers to the temporary experiences of bliss, clarity, and nonthought produced through meditation practice. Specifically, one of the three stages: intellectual understanding, experience, and realization.

EXPRESSION MANIFEST IN MANIFOLD WAYS (rtsal sna tshogs su snang ba) The third of the three aspects of sugatagarbha: essence, nature, expression.

EXTREME OF ETERNALISM (rtag mtha') *See* Eternalism.

EXTREME OF NIHILISM (chad mtha') *See* Nihilism.

FABRICATED ATTRIBUTES (spros mtshan) Characteristics such as arising and ceasing, singularity or plurality, coming and going, permanence and annihilation, which are falsely attributed to the nature of things or to sugatagarbha.

FIRST DHYANA (bsam gtan dang po) One of the four domains

Glossary

in the realm of form, the causes of which are produced through a meditation state of the same name.

FIVE AGGREGATES *See* Five skandhas.

FIVE BODHISATTVA PATHS (byang chub sems dpa'i lam lnga) *See* Five paths.

FIVE ELEMENTS (khams/'byung ba lnga) Earth, water, fire, wind, and space.

FIVE EYES (spyan lnga) The physical eye, the divine eye, the eye of discriminating knowledge, the eye of dharma, and the eye of wisdom (also called "buddha-eye").

FIVE FACULTIES (dbang po lnga) The five faculties "ruling" over the first two of the four aspects of ascertainment on the path of joining: faith, mindfulness, diligence, concentration, and discriminating knowledge.

FIVE MAJOR ROOT PRANAS (rtsa ba'i rlung chen lnga) The winds circulating within the human body, which have the nature of the five elements: the life-upholding, the downward-clearing, the upward-moving, the equally-abiding, and the pervading wind.

FIVE MINOR BRANCH PRANAS (yan lag gi lung phran lnga)

FIVE PATHS (lam lnga) The paths of accumulation, joining, seeing, cultivation, and no-learning. The five paths cover the entire process from beginning dharma practice to complete enlightenment.

FIVE SKANDHAS (phung po lnga) The five aspects or "aggregates" that comprise the physical and mental constituents of a sentient being: physical forms, sensations, conceptions, (mental) formations, and consciousnesses.

FIVE STRENGTHS (stobs lnga) Similar to the five ruling faculties but differing in that they have become indomitable by adverse factors. They cover the last two of the four aspects of ascertainment on the path of joining.

FIVE SUPERKNOWLEDGES (mngon shes lnga) The capacities for performing miracles, divine sight, divine hearing, recollection of former lives, and cognition of the minds of others.

FORMLESS REALM (gzugs med kyi khams) *See* Four formless realms.

Glossary

FORTY THOUGHT STATES RESULTING FROM DESIRE *See* Eighty inherent thought states.

FOUR APPLICATIONS OF MINDFULNESS (dran pa nye bar bzhag pa bzhi) Mindfulness of the body, sensations, mind, and phenomena. Their essence being discriminating knowledge concurrent with mindfulness, they are chiefly practiced on the lesser stage of the path of accumulation.

FOUR ASPECTS OF ASCERTAINMENT (nges 'byed kyi yan lag bzhi) *See* Four aspects of the path of joining.

FOUR ASPECTS OF THE PATH OF JOINING ('byor lam gyi yan lag bzhi) Heat, summit, acceptance, and supreme attribute. For details see each individually.

FOUR DOMAINS OF THE REALM OF FORM (gzugs khams kyi gnas ris bzhi) The abodes of beings who have cultivated the meditative states of the four dhyanas.

FOUR FORMLESS REALMS (gzugs med kyi khams bzhi) The abode of an unenlightened being who has practiced the four absorptions—the four unenlightened meditative states of dwelling on the thoughts: infinite space, infinite consciousness, nothing whatsoever, and neither presence nor absence [of conception]. The formless realm is one of the "three realms."

FOUR FORMLESS SPHERES OF FINALITY (gzugs med kyi skye mched mu bzhi) *See* Four formless realms.

FOUR JOYS (dga' bzhi) Joy, supreme joy, nonjoy, and innate joy.

FOUR KAYAS (sku bzhi) The three kayas plus svabhavikakaya. *See* Three kayas; Svabhavikakaya.

FOUR LEGS OF MIRACULOUS ACTION (rdzu 'phrul gyi rkang pa bzhi) Determination, discernment, diligence, and samadhi; perfected on the greater path of accumulation.

FOUR LEVELS OF EMPTINESS (stong pa bzhi) Emptiness, special emptiness, great emptiness, universal emptiness.

FOUR RIGHT EXERTIONS (yang dag spong ba bzhi) To avoid giving rise to nonvirtuous qualities, to abandon the ones that have arisen, to give rise to virtuous qualities, and to avoid letting the ones that have arisen degenerate. They are perfected on the medium stage of the path of accumulation.

FOUR SECTIONS OF TANTRA (rgyud sde bzhi) Kriya, charya, yoga, and anuttara yoga.

Glossary

FOUR VISIONS OF DZOGCHEN (rdzogs chen gyi snang ba bzhi) Four stages in dzogchen practice: manifest dharmata, increased experience, awareness reaching fullness, and exhaustion of concepts and phenomena.

FOUR YOGAS (rnal 'byor bzhi) *See* Four yogas of mahamudra.

FOUR YOGAS OF MAHAMUDRA (phyag chen gyi rnal 'byor bzhi) Four stages in mahamudra practice: one-pointedness, simplicity, one taste, and nonmeditation.

FOURTH EMPOWERMENT OF MANTRA (sngags kyi dbang bzhi pa) Also called the "precious word empowerment" (tshig dbang rin po che), the purpose of which is to point out the nature of mind.

FORTY THOUGHT STATES RESULTING FROM DESIRE ('dod chags las byung ba'i rtog pa bzhi bcu) *See* Eighty inherent thought states.

FRUITION MAHAMUDRA ('bras bu phyag chen) The state of complete and perfect buddhahood.

GAMPO MOUNTAIN (sgam po ri) Lord Gampopa's seat in Central Tibet.

GARUDA (mkha' lding) The mythological bird, able to travel with a single movement of its wings from one end of the universe to the other.

GATHERING THE ACCUMULATIONS (tshogs bsags pa) The virtuous practices of perfecting the "two accumulations" of merit and wisdom.

GENERAL GROUND OF SAMSARA AND NIRVANA ('khor 'das kyi spyi gzhi)

GENERAL PRELIMINARIES (thun mong gi sngon 'gro) The four contemplations on precious human body, impermanence and death, cause and effect of karma, and the defects of samsara.

GENERAL SECRET MANTRA (gsang sngags spyi) The first three of the "four sections of tantra."

GENERAL VEHICLES (thun mong gi theg pa) Hinayana and mahayana. Synonymous with *common vehicles*.

GOD REALMS (lha ris) Six abodes of the gods of the desire realm; seventeen abodes of the gods of the realm of form, and four abodes of the gods of the formless realm.

Glossary

GOOD INTELLIGENCE (legs pa'i blo gros) The ninth of the ten bhumis.

GRADUAL TYPE (rim gyis pa) A practitioner taking the gradual approach to enlightenment.

GREAT BRAHMIN (bram ze chen po) *See* Saraha.

GREAT DARKNESS OF BEGINNINGLESS TIME (thog med dus kyi mun pa chen po) Primordial ignorance perpetuated in the minds of sentient beings.

Great Pacifying River Tantra (zhi byed chu bo chen po'i rgyud)

GROUND MAHAMUDRA (gzhi phyag chen)

GROUP CONDUCT (tshogs spyod) One of the numerous types of conduct.

Guhyagarbha Tantra (rgyud gsang ba snying po) The widely renowned mahayoga tantra of the Old School of the Early Translations. *See* Gyurme Dorje's forthcoming translation.

GUHYAMANTRA (gsang sngags) Synonymous with *vajrayana* or tantric teachings. "Guhya" means secret, both concealed and self-secret. "Mantra" in this context means eminent, excellent, or praiseworthy. Synonymous with *secret mantra.*

GURU RINPOCHE (gu ru rin po che) The "Precious Master," refers to Padmakara, Padmasambhava.

GURU YOGA (bla ma'i rnal 'byor) The practice of supplicating for the blessings and mingling the mind of an enlightened master with one's own mind. One of the special inner preliminaries.

GYALWA LO-RE (rgyal ba lo ras) *See* Lorepa.

HABITUAL TENDENCIES (bag chags) Subtle inclinations imprinted in the all-ground consciousness.

HARD TO CONQUER (sbyang dka' ba) The fifth of the ten bhumis.

HEAT (drod) The first of the "four aspects of ascertainment" on the path of joining. Getting close to the flamelike wisdom of the path of seeing by possessing concentration concurrent with discriminating knowledge.

HINAYANA (theg pa dman pa) The vehicles focused on contemplation of the four noble truths and the twelve links of dependent origination for the sake of individual liberation.

IGNORANT ASPECT OF THE ALL-GROUND (kun gzhi ma rig pa'i cha)   Synonymous with *coemergent ignorance.*

INEXHAUSTIBLE ADORNMENT WHEEL OF BODY, SPEECH, AND MIND (sku gsung thugs mi zad pa rgyan gyi 'khor lo)

INFINITE CONSCIOUSNESS (rnam shes mtha' yas)   The second abode in the formless realm dwelling on the thought, "Consciousness is infinite!"

INFINITE SPACE (nam mkha' mtha' yas)   The first abode in the formless realm dwelling on the thought, "Space is infinite!"

INSEPARABILITY OF THE THREE KAYAS (sku gsum dbyer med)

INSTANTANEOUS TYPE (cig car ba'i rigs)   The type of person who does not need to go through progressive stages on the path.

INTELLECTUAL UNDERSTANDING (go ba)   First step of three: understanding, experience, and realization.

JOYOUS (rab tu dga' ba)   The first of the ten bhumis.

KAGYU (bka' brgyud)   The teachings received from the dharmakaya buddha Vajradhara by the Indian siddha Tilopa, Saraha, and others. Transmitted by Naropa and Maitripa to the Tibetan translator Marpa, the lineage was gradually passed on to Milarepa, Gampopa, Karmapa, and others. The main emphasis is on the path of means, which is the Six Yogas of Naropa, and the path of liberation, which is the mahamudra instructions of Maitripa. In addition to these teachings, Gampopa also received the Kadampa teachings on mind training brought to Tibet by Lord Atisha, which he fused into one system now renowned as the Dakpo Kagyu. It is from the chief disciples of Lord Gampopa that the four great and eight lesser lineages trace their sources. For more details, read *Rain of Wisdom* and *The Life of Marpa the Translator* (both from Shambhala Publications).

KA-NYING SHEDRUP LING MONASTERY (bka' snying bshad sgrub gling)   Tulku Chökyi Nyima Rinpoche's monastery in

Glossary

Boudhanath, Nepal. The name means "sanctuary for Kagyu and Nyingma teaching and practice."

KAYA (sku) "Body" in the sense of a body or embodiment of numerous qualities.

KAYAS AND WISDOMS (sku dang ye shes) The four kayas and five wisdoms.

King of Samadhi Sutra (ting 'dzin rgyal po'i mdo) A sutra belonging to the third turning of the wheel of the dharma.

KNOWLEDGE (shes rab) *See* Means and knowledge.

LAMDRE (lam 'bras) "Path and fruition/result." The main teaching of the Sakya school.

Lankavatara Sutra (lang kar gshegs pa'i mdo) A sutra of the third turning of the wheel of the dharma. Used as basis for Yogachara and Chittamatra.

LIBERATING INSTRUCTIONS (grol byed kyi khrid) Oral instructions received from an authentic master which, when practiced, liberate one's mind from delusion.

LIBERATION (thar pa) Emancipation from samsaric existence.

LORD DA-Ö SHÖNNU (rje zla 'od gzhon nu) Chandrakumara, another of Gampopa's names.

LORD GAMPOPA (rje btsun sgam po pa) The great father of all the Kagyu lineages. For details see *The Life of Milarepa* and *The Rain of Wisdom* (both from Shambhala Publications).

LOREPA (lo ras pa) A great lineage master in the Drukpa Kagyu school.

LOTUS OF NONATTACHMENT (ma chags pad ma) The twelfth bhumi.

LOWER TANTRAS OF MANTRA (sngags kyi rgyud 'og ma) The three sections of tantra: kriya, charya, and yoga.

LOWER VEHICLES (theg pa 'og ma) Compared to vajrayana, the lower are the vehicles of shravakas, pratyekabuddhas, and bodhisattvas.

LUMINOSITIES OF MOTHER AND CHILD ('od gsal ma bu) "Mother luminosity" is the buddha nature inherent in all beings. "Child luminosity" is the recognition of that which one's teacher points out.

91

Glossary

LUMINOSITY ('od gsal) Free from the darkness of unknowing and endowed with the ability to cognize. The two aspects are "empty luminosity," like a clear open sky, and "manifest luminosity," such as five-colored lights, images, and so forth. Luminosity is the uncompounded nature present throughout all of samsara and nirvana.

LUMINOUS WISDOM OF DHARMATA (chos nyid 'od gsal gyi ye shes)

MACHIK LABDRÖN (ma gcig lab sgron) The great female master who set down the chö practice.

MAHASANDHI (rdzogs pa chen po) Literally, "great perfection," the most direct practice for realizing one's buddha nature, according to the Nyingma or Old School. *See also* Dzogchen.

MAHAYANA (theg pa chen po) The vehicle of bodhisattvas striving for perfect enlightenment for the sake of all beings. For a detailed explanation, see Maitreya's *Abhisamayalamkara*.

MAIN PART OF PRACTICE (nyams len gyi dngos gzhi) Refers to the practice that follows the preliminaries: either yidam practice or, in this case, the actual practice of mahamudra.

MAITREYA (byams pa) The "Loving One," the bodhisattva regent of Buddha Shakyamuni, presently residing in the Tushita heaven until he becomes the fifth buddha of this kalpa.

MANIBHADRA (nor bzang) A great bodhisattva of a past aeon.

MANTRA MAHAMUDRA (sngags kyi phyag chen) The mahamudra practice connected to the six doctrines of Naropa. *See* Tulku Urgyen Rinpoche's "Introduction."

MARKS AND SIGNS (mtshan dpe) A perfect buddha's thirty-two major and eighty minor marks of excellence.

MEANS AND KNOWLEDGE (thabs dang shes rab, prajna and upaya) Generally, buddhahood is attained by uniting the two aspects of means and knowledge, in mahayana compassion and emptiness, and in vajrayana the stages of development and completion. According to the Kagyu schools in particular, these two aspects are the "path of means," referring to the six doctrines and the "path of liberation," referring to the actual practice of mahamudra.

Glossary

MEDITATION (sgom pa) In the context of mahamudra practice, meditation is "the act of growing accustomed" or "sustaining the continuity."

MEDITATION AND POSTMEDITATION (mnyam bzhag dang rjes thob) "Meditation" here means resting in equanimity free from mental constructs. "Postmeditation" is when distracted from that state of equanimity. *See also* Postmeditation.

MENTAL CONSTRUCTS (spros pa)

MIND CONSCIOUSNESS (yid kyi rnam par shes pa) According to abhidharma, one of the eight consciousness. Its function is to discriminate and label things.

MIND-ESSENCE (sems nyid) The nature of one's mind, which is taught to be identical with the essence of all enlightened beings, the sugatagarbha. It should be distinguished from "mind" (sems), which refers to ordinary discursive thinking based on ignorance of the nature of thought.

MIND-STREAM (sems rgyud) Individual continuity of cognition.

MIRACULOUS POWERS (rdzu 'phrul)

MUNDANE DHYANA ('jig rten pa'i bsam gtan) A meditation state characterized by attachment, especially to bliss, clarity, and nonthought, and lacking insight into the emptiness of a self-entity.

MUNDANE SAMADHIS ('jig rten pa'i ting nge 'dzin) Similar to *mundane dhyana.*

NADI, PRANA, AND BINDU (rtsa rlung thig le) The channels, energies or winds, and essences of the physical body.

NAGARJUNA (klu grub) An Indian master of philosophy.

NAGI GOMPA (na gi dgon pa) Tulku Urgyen Rinpoche's hermitage near Kathmandu.

NAKED ORDINARY MIND (tha mal gyi shes pa rjen pa)

NAMO MAHAMUDRAYE (Skt.) "Homage to mahamudra," the great seal.

NAROPA (na ro pa) The chief disciple of Tilupa and the guru of Marpa in the Kagyu lineage.

NATURAL FACE OF DHARMAKAYA (chos sku'i rang zhal)

Glossary

NATURAL FACE OF GROUND MAHAMUDRA (gzhi phyag chen gyi rang zhal)

NATURAL FACE OF MIND (sems nyid rang zhal)

NEITHER PRESENCE NOR ABSENCE [OF CONCEPTIONS] (['du shes] yod min med min)   The third abode in the formless realm, dwelling on the thought "My perception is neither absent nor present!"

Nekyi Sintig (gnad kyi zin tig)   A scripture on mahamudra.

NEW SCHOOLS (gsar ma)   *See* Old and New Schools.

NIGUMA (ni gu ma)   A great female Indian master and a teacher of Khyungpo Naljor.

NIHILISM (chad lta)   Literally "the view of discontinuance." The extreme view of nothingness: no rebirth or karmic effects and the nonexistence of a mind after death.

NINE DHYANAS OF ABSORPTION (snyoms 'jug gi bsam gtan dgu)   The four dhyanas, the four formless states, and the shravaka's samadhi of peace.

NIRMANAKAYA (sprul sku)   "Emanation body," the third of the three kayas. The aspect of enlightenment that tames and can be perceived by ordinary beings. *See also* Three kayas.

NIRVANA (mya ngan las 'das pa)   The lesser nirvana refers to the liberation from cyclic existence attained by a hinayana practitioner. When referring to a buddha, nirvana is the great nondwelling state of enlightenment, which falls neither into the extreme of samsaric existence nor into the passive state of cessation attained by an arhant.

NONARISING ESSENCE (gshis skye ba med pa)

NONCONCEPTUAL WAKEFULNESS (rnam par mi rtog pa'i ye shes)

NONCONCEPTUAL WISDOM (rnam par mi rtog pa'i ye shes)

NONDISTRACTION (g.yengs med)   Not straying from the continuity of the practice.

NONFABRICATION (bzo med)

NONFIXATION (sgom med)   The state of not holding on to subject and object.

NONMEDITATION ('dzin med)   The state of not holding on to an object meditated upon nor a subject who meditates. Also refers to the fourth stage of mahamudra in which nothing further needs to be meditated upon or cultivated.

NOTHING WHATSOEVER (ci yang med pa)   The third of the four formless realms in which one dwells on the thought, "Nothing whatsoever!"

NYINGMA TRADITION (rnying lugs)   The teachings brought to Tibet and translated chiefly during the reign of King Trisong Detsen and in the following period up to Rinchen Sangpo.

OBSCURATION OF DUALISTIC KNOWLEDGE (shes bya'i sgrib pa)   The subtle obscuration of holding on to the concepts of subject, object, and action.

OBSCURATIONS (sgrib pa)   The veils that cover one's direct perception of the nature of mind. In the general Buddhist teachings several types are mentioned: the obscuration of karma preventing one from entering the path of enlightenment, the obscuration of disturbing emotions preventing progress along the path, the obscuration of habitual tendencies preventing the vanishing of confusion, and the final obscuration of dualistic knowledge preventing the full attainment of buddhahood.

OLD AND NEW SCHOOLS (rnying ma dang gsar ma)   Although there were no new or old schools in India, these names refer to the early and later spread of the teachings in Tibet. Translations up to and including King Triral are called the Old School of Early Translations (snga 'gyur snying ma), and later ones are known as the New Schools of Later Translations (phyi 'gyur gsar ma). The Old School is the Nyingma tradition. Lochen Rinchen Sangpo (lo chen rin chen bzang po) is regarded as the first translator of the New Mantra School. The New Schools are the Kagyu, Sakya, and Gelug.

OMNISCIENCE (rnam mkhyen, thams cad mkhyen pa)   Same as complete enlightenment or buddhahood.

ONE-POINTEDNESS (rtse gcig)   The first stage in the practice of mahamudra.

ONE TASTE (ro gcig)   The third stage in the practice of mahamudra.

Glossary

Openness of Realization Tantra (dgongs pa zang thal gyi rgyud) A tantric scripture concealed by Guru Rinpoche and revealed by Rigdzin Godem, the master who revealed the Jangter tradition of the Nyingma school. Contains the renowned "Aspiration of Samantabhadra."

PARAMITA VEHICLE (phar phyin gyi theg pa) The sutra system of the gradual path through the five paths and ten bhumis according to the prajnaparamita scriptures.

PATH MAHAMUDRA (lam phyag rgya chen po) The stage of approaching the recognition of the sugatagarbha and of applying that recognition in one's practice.

PATH OF ACCUMULATION (tshogs lam) The first of the five paths, which emphasizes the accumulation of merit, faith, and mindfulness.

PATH OF CULTIVATION (sgom lam) The fourth of the five paths on which one cultivates and trains in the higher practices of a bodhisattva, especially the eight aspects of the path of noble beings.

PATH OF FULFILLMENT (mthar phyin pa'i lam) Synonymous with the *path of no-learning.*

PATH OF JOINING (sbyor lam) The second of the five paths on which one grows closer to and joins with the realization of the truth of reality.

PATH OF LIBERATION (grol lam) The path of mahamudra practice.

PATH OF NO-LEARNING (mi slob pa'i lam) The fifth of the five paths and the state of complete and perfect enlightenment.

PATH OF SEEING (mthong lam) The third of the five paths, which is the attainment of the first bhumi, liberation from samsara, and realization of the truth of reality.

PATHS AND BHUMIS (sa lam) The five paths and the ten bodhisattva levels.

PATHS OF LEARNING (slob pa'i lam) The first four of the five paths on which concepts of progress, training, and learning still remain.

PERFECT BUDDHAHOOD (rdzogs pa'i sangs rgyas) The extinction

Glossary

of all faults and obscurations and the perfection of all enlightened qualities.

PERMANENT OR ANNIHILATED (rtag pa dang chad pa) Lasting forever as in an eternalistic point of view or ceasing to exist as in a nihilistic view.

PERSONAL EXPERIENCE (rang snang) Exemplified by the dream experience, this term is sometimes translated as "one's own projection" or "self-display."

PERSONAL MANIFESTATION (rang snang) Synonymous with *personal experience*.

PHENOMENA (chos, snang ba) Anything that can be experienced, thought of, or known.

PHILOSOPHICAL SCHOOLS (grub mtha') The four Buddhist schools of thought: Vaibhashika, Sautrantika, Chittamatra, and Madhyamaka. The former two are hinayana and the latter mahayana.

POSTMEDITATION (rjes thob) Generally, the period of involvement in sense perception and activities. Specifically, the time when distracted from the natural state of mind. *See also* Meditation and postmeditation.

PRACTICE LINEAGE (sgrub brgyud) The lineage of masters who emphasize one's personal experience of the teachings as opposed to the scholastic lineage of expounding the scriptures (bshad brgyud). *See* Eight Practice Lineages.

PRAJNAPARAMITA (shes rab kyi pha rol tu phyin pa) "Transcendent knowledge," the mahayana teachings on insight into emptiness, transcending the fixation of subject, object, and action.

PRANA (rlung) See Nadi, prana, and bindu.

PRANA-MIND (rlung sems) *Prana* here is the wind of karma and "mind" is the dualistic consciousness of an unenlightened being.

PRATYEKABUDDHA (rang sangs rgyas) "Solitarily Enlightened One," one who has reached perfection in the second hinayana vehicle, chiefly through contemplation on the twelve links of dependent origination in reverse order.

PRECIOUS WORD EMPOWERMENT (tshig dbang rin po che) *See* Fourth empowerment of mantra.

Glossary

PRELIMINARIES (sngon 'gro) The general outer preliminaries are the four mind-changings; the special inner preliminaries are the four times hundred-thousand practices of refuge and bodhichitta, Vajrasattva recitation, mandala offering, and guru yoga. For details, see *The Torch of Certainty* (Shambhala Publications, 1977) and *The Great Gate* (Rangjung Yeshe Publications, 1989).

PURIFYING THE OBSCURATIONS (sgrib sbyong) The spiritual practices of clearing away what obscures the sugatagarbha, for example, the meditation and recitation of Vajrasattva according to the special preliminaries.

QUALIFIED MASTER (bla ma mtshan nyid dang ldan pa) Someone with the correct view and genuine compassion. For details see *Kindly Bent to Ease Us,* vol. 1 (Dharma Publishing, 1975).

RADIANT ('od byed pa) The third of the ten bhumis.

RAINBOW BODY ('ja' lus) At the time of death of a practitioner who has reached the exhaustion of all grasping and fixation, the five gross elements that form the physical body dissolve back into their essences, five-colored light. Sometimes the hair and the nails alone are left behind.

REACHING FAR (ring du song ba) The seventh of the ten bhumis.

REALIZATION (rtogs pa) The third stage in the sequence of understanding, experience, and realization.

REALIZED (mngon du gyur pa) The sixth of the ten bhumis.

REALIZING THE VIEW (lta ba rtogs pa)

REALM OF FORM (gzugs kyi khams) One of the "three realms," the seventeen samsaric heavenly abodes consisting of the threefold four dhyana realms and the five pure abodes. The beings there have bodies of light, long lives, and no painful sensations.

RESULTANT SECRET MANTRA ('bras bu gsang sngags) The vajra-yana system of taking the fruition as the path as opposed to the causal philosophical vehicles. *See also* Secret mantra.

RIPENING EMPOWERMENTS (smin byed kyi dbang) The vajra-

Glossary

yana empowerments, which ripen one's being with the capacity to realize the four kayas.

ROYAL SEAT OF DHARMAKAYA (chos sku'i rgyal sa)   Synonymous with complete buddhahood.

ROYAL THRONE OF THE THREE KAYAS (sku gsum gyi btsan sa) Synonymous with complete buddhahood.

RUPAKAYA (gzugs kyi sku)   "Form body," a collective term for both sambhogakaya and nirmanakaya.

SADAPRARUDITA (rtag tu ngu)   The "Ever-Weeping" bodhisattva of a past aeon used as an example for unwavering devotion and perseverance. He is mentioned in the prajnaparamita scriptures.

SAMADHI (ting nge 'dzin)   "Adhering to continuity or evenness."

SAMADHI OF COURAGEOUS MOVEMENT (dpa' bar 'gro ba'i ting nge 'dzin)   The shurangama samadhi described in the *Shurangama Sutra*.

SAMADHI OF MAGICAL ILLUSION (sgyu 'phrul gyi ting nge 'dzin)

SAMADHI OF THE FIRST DHYANA (bsam gtan dang po'i ting nge 'dzin)   *See* First dhyana.

SAMADHI OF THE MAJESTIC LION (seng ge bsgyings pa'i ting nge 'dzin)   Described in *The Flower Ornament Scripture*, vol. 3 (Shambhala Publications, 1987).

SAMAYA (dam tshig)   The sacred pledge, precepts, or commitment of vajrayana practice. Many details exists, but the samayas essentially consist of: outwardly, maintaining harmonious relationship with the vajra master and one's dharma friends and inwardly, not straying from the continuity of the practice.

SAMBHOGAKAYA (longs spyod rdzogs pa'i sku)   The "body of perfect enjoyment." Of the five kayas of fruition, this is the semimanifest form of the buddhas endowed with the five perfections of perfect teacher, retinue, place, teaching, and time, which is perceptible only to bodhisattvas on the ten bhumis. *See also* Three kayas.

SAMENESS OF SPACE AND WISDOM (dbyings dang ye shes mnyam pa nyid)

Glossary

SAMSARA ('khor ba) "Cyclic existence," "vicious circle," or "round" of births and deaths. The state of ordinary sentient beings fettered by ignorance and dualistic perception, karma, and disturbing emotions.

SAMSARA AND NIRVANA ('khor 'das) Pure and impure phenomena.

SARAHA (sa ra ha) One of the mahasiddhas of India and a master in the mahamudra lineage; known as the Great Brahmin. For details see Herbert V. Guenther, trans., *The Royal Song of Saraha* (Shambhala Publications, 1973).

SECRET CONDUCT (gsang ba'i spyod pa) One of the different types of conduct used as an enhancement practice.

SECRET MANTRA (gsang sngags, guhyamantra) Synonymous with *vajrayana*. *See also* Guhyamantra.

SEEING THE MIND-ESSENCE (sems ngo mthong ba)

SELF-AWARE SELF-COGNIZANCE (rang rig rang gsal)

SELF-COGNIZANT MINDFULNESS (rang gsal gyi dran pa)

SELF-ENTITY (rang bzhin) An inherently existent and independent entity of the individual self or of phenomena.

SELF-EXISTING NATURAL FLOW (rang byung rang babs)

SELF-EXISTING SELF-COGNIZANCE (rang byung rang gsal)

SELF-EXISTING WISDOM (rang byung ye shes) Basic wakefulness independent of intellectual constructs.

SEVEN ASPECTS OF UNION (kha sbyor yan lag bdun) The seven qualities of a sambhogakaya buddha: complete enjoyment, union, great bliss, absence of a self-nature, presence of compassion, being uninterrupted, and being unceasing.

SEVEN BODHI-FACTORS (byang chub yan lag bdun) Samadhi, full discernment of phenomena, mindfulness, diligence, joy, pliancy, impartiality.

SEVEN THOUGHT STATES RESULTING FROM DELUSION (gti mug las byung ba'i rtog pa bdun) *See* Eighty inherent thought states.

Seven Wheels of Kshitigarbha Sutra (sa snying 'khor lo bdun gyi mdo)

SHAMATHA (zhi gnas) "Calm abiding" or "remaining in quiescence" after the subsiding of thought activity or the medita-

Glossary

tive practice of calming the mind in order to rest free from the disturbance of thought.

SHAMATHA CESSATION (zhi gnas 'gog pa) In the context of vajrayana practice, this term is used in a derogative sense and is renowned as a severe sidetrack from the path of enlightenment. The mistake comes from regarding meditation practice as being the act of cultivating and fixating on a state in which sensations and thoughts are absent.

SHAMATHA THAT DELIGHTS THE TATHAGATAS (de bzhin gshegs dgyes/ dge'i zhi gnas) The shamatha state at the first bhumi, which is embraced with insight into emptiness.

SHAMATHA WITH ATTRIBUTES (mtshan bcas zhi gnas)

SHAMATHA WITH SUPPORT (zhi gnas rten bcas)

SHAMATHA WITHOUT ATTRIBUTES (mtshan med zhi gnas)

SHAMATHA WITHOUT SUPPORT (zhi gnas rten med)

SHIJE (zhi byed) "Pacifying," one of the Eight Practice Lineages, brought to Tibet by Phadampa Sangye.

SHRAVAKA (nyan thos) "Hearer" or "listener," the practitioners of the first turning of the wheel of the dharma on the four noble truths.

SHRAVAKA'S SAMADHI OF PEACE (nyan thos kyi zhi ba'i ting nge 'dzin)

SIDDHA (grub thob) "Accomplished one," someone who has attained siddhi; an accomplished master.

SIDDHI (dngos grub) "Accomplishment," usually refers to the "supreme siddhi" of complete enlightenment, but can also mean the "common siddhis," eight mundane accomplishments.

SIMPLICITY (spros bral) The second stage in the practice of mahamudra.

SINGLE CIRCLE OF DHARMAKAYA (chos sku thig le nyag cig)

SINGLE SUFFICIENT JEWEL (nor bu gcig chog) The personal teacher regarded as the embodiment of the three jewels, the three roots, and the three kayas.

SIX CLASSES OF BEINGS ('gro ba rigs drug) Gods, demigods, human beings, animals, hungry ghosts, and hell beings.

SIX COLLECTIONS [OF CONSCIOUSNESS] ([rnam shes] tshogs

drug) The five sense consciousnesses and the mind consciousness.

SIX DOCTRINES OF NAROPA (chos drug) Tummo, illusory body, dream, luminosity, bardo, and phowa. *See also* Means and knowledge.

SIX ORNAMENTS AND THE TWO SUPREME ONES (rgyan drug mchog gnyis) The six ornaments are Nagarjuna, Aryadeva, Asanga, Dignaga, Vasubhandu, and Dharmakirti. The two supreme ones are Shakyaprabha and Gunaprabha.

SKANDHAS (phung po) *See* Five skandhas.

SKIPPING THE GRADES TYPE (thod rgal ba'i rigs) People whose qualities of experience and realization increase and decrease without sequential order.

SOGLUNG (srog rlung) An illness caused by prana getting stuck in the heart center due to various strenuous circumstances.

SPECIAL PRELIMINARIES (thun min gyi sngon 'gro) Taking refuge, arousing bodhicitta, recitation and meditation of Vajrasattva, mandala offerings, and guru yoga. For further details see *The Torch of Certainty* (Shambhala Publications, 1977) or *The Great Gate* (Rangjung Yeshe Publications, 1989).

STAINLESS (dri ma med pa) The second of the ten bhumis.

STILLNESS (gnas pa) Absence of thought activity and disturbing emotions, but with subtle fixation on this stillness. .

SUCHNESS (de bzhin nyid) Synonym for emptiness or the nature of things, dharmata; it can also be used to describe the unity of dependent origination and emptiness.

SUGATA-ESSENCE (bde gshegs snying po) Another word for buddha-nature, the enlightened essence inherent in sentient beings.

SUGATAGARBHA (bde bar gshegs pa'i snying po) "Sugata-essence," the most common Sanskrit term for what in the West is known as "buddha nature."

SUMERU (ri rab) The mountain in the center of the four continents.

SUMMIT (rtse mo) One of the four aspects of ascertainment on the path of joining.

SUPERKNOWLEDGES (mngon par shes pa) *See* Five superknowledges.

Glossary

SUPREME ATTRIBUTE (chos mchog) The fourth of the four aspects of ascertainment on the path of joining. The highest spiritual attainment within samsaric existence.

SUPREME MUNDANE QUALITY ('jig rten chos mchog) Synonymous with *supreme attribute*.

SUTRA (mdo) Discourse or teaching by the Buddha. Also refers to all the causal teachings that take the cause as the path as a whole. This includes the teachings of both hinayana and mahayana.

SUTRA AND TANTRA (mdo rgyud) *See* Sutra; Tantra.

SUTRA MAHAMUDRA (mdo'i phyag chen) The mahamudra system based on the prajnaparamita scriptures and emphasizing shamatha and vipashyana and the progressive journey through the five paths and ten bodhisattva bhumis.

SUTRA SYSTEM (mdo lugs) Refers in this context to the progressive bodhisattva path.

SVABHAVIKAKAYA (ngo bo nyid kyi sku) The "essence body," sometimes counted as the fourth kaya, the unity of the first three.

SYMBOLIC WISDOM (dpe'i ye shes) The wisdom which is the unity of bliss and emptiness of the third empowerment and which is used to introduce the true wisdom of the fourth empowerment.

TAKNYI TANTRA (rgyud brtags pa gnyis pa) The short version of the *Hevajra Tantra*.

TANTRA (rgyud) The vajrayana teachings given by the Buddha in his sambhogakaya form. Literally "continuity," tantra means the buddha nature, the tantra of the expressed meaning. Generally, the extraordinary tantric scriptures, which are exalted above the sutras, the tantra of the expressing words. Can also refer to all the resultant teachings that take the result as the path.

Tantra of the Inconceivable Secret (gsang ba bsam gyis mi khyab pa'i rgyud) A tantra of the New Schools, which sets forth the system of mahamudra.

TATHAGATA (de bzhin gshegs pa) "Thus-gone," a fully enlightened buddha. The buddhas who have gone (gata) to the state

Glossary

of dharmata or suchness (tatha). Synonym for sugata and jina.

TEMPORARY STAINS (glo bur gyi dri ma). The obscurations that are not intrinsic to the sugatagarbha, like clouds are not inherent in the sky.

TEMPORARY STRAYING FROM THE ESSENCE (gshis kyi 'phral shor)

TEMPORARY STRAYING FROM THE PATH (lam gyi 'phral shor)

TEMPORARY STRAYING FROM THE REMEDY (gnyen po 'phral shor)

TEMPORARY STRAYING INTO GENERALIZING (rgyas 'debs 'phral shor)

TEN BHUMIS (sa bcu) The ten bodhisattva levels or stages: the joyous, the stainless, the radiant, the brilliant, the hard to conquer, the realized, the reaching far, the unshakable, the good intelligence, and the cloud of dharma. These ten stages are included in the last three of the five paths.

THINKING AND STILLNESS (gnas 'gyu) Presence and absence of thought activity.

THIRD EMPOWERMENT (dbang gsum pa) The third of the four empowerments in the anuttara yoga system, which introduces the unity of bliss and emptiness.

THIRTY-FIVE THOUGHT STATES RESULTING FROM ANGER (zhe sdang las byung ba'i rtog pa so gsum) See Eighty inherent thought states.

THOUGHT ARISING AS MEDITATION (rnam rtog bsgom du 'char ba)

THREE GATES OF EMANCIPATION (rnam thar sgo gsum) Emptiness, marklessness, and wishlessness.

THREE JEWELS (dkon mchog gsum) The precious buddha, the precious dharma, and the precious sangha.

THREE KAYAS (sku gsum) Dharmakaya, sambhogakaya, and nirmanakaya. The three kayas as ground are "essence, nature, and expression," as path they are "bliss, clarity, and non-thought," and as fruition they are the "three kayas of buddhahood." See also Dharmakaya; Sambhogakaya; Nirmanakaya.

THREE KAYAS OF BUDDHAHOOD (sangs rgyas sku gsum) The dharmakaya is free from elaborate constructs and endowed with the twenty-one sets of enlightened qualities. Sambho-

104

Glossary

gakaya is of the nature of light and endowed with the perfect major and minor marks, perceptible only to bodhisattvas on the bhumis. The nirmanakaya manifests in forms perceptible to both pure and impure beings.

THREE NATURES (rang bzhin gsum/ mtshan nyid gsum) The aspects of phenomena as set forth by the Chittamatra and Yogachara schools; the imagined, the dependent, and the absolute. The imagined (kun brtags) is the two kinds of self-entity. The dependent (gzhan dbang) is the eight collections of consciousness. The absolute (yongs grub) is the empty nature of things, suchness.

THREE REALMS (khams gsum) The samsaric realms of desire, form, and formlessness. *See also* Desire realm; Four Formless Realms; Realm of form.

THREE ROOTS (rtsa ba gsum) Guru, yidam, and dakini. The guru is the root of blessings, the yidam is the root of accomplishment, and the dakini is the root of activity.

THREEFOLD PURITY ('khor gsum rnam dag) Absence of fixation on subject, object, and action.

TILOPA (ti lo pa) Indian mahasiddha, the guru of Naropa, and father of the Kagyu lineage.

TIRTHIKA (mu stegs pa) Non-Buddhist teachers of philosophy adhering to the extreme views of eternalism or nihilism.

TRANSCENDENT KNOWLEDGE (shes rab kyi pha rol tu phyin pa, prajnaparamita) Intelligence that transcends conceptual thinking.

TREKCHÖ (khregs chod) "Cutting through." One of the two main aspects of dzogchen practice, the other being thögal. *See also* Cutting through.

TRUE ALL-GROUND OF APPLICATION (sbyor ba don gyi kun gzhi)

TRUE WISDOM (don gyi ye shes) The wisdom which is the unity of awareness and emptiness introduced through the fourth empowerment.

TULKU URGYEN RINPOCHE (sprul sku u rgyan rin po che) A contemporary master of the Kagyu and Nyingma lineages, who lives at Nagi Gompa in Nepal.

TWELVE-TIMES-ONE-HUNDRED QUALITIES (yon tan brgya phrag

bcu gnyis) At the level of the first bodhisattva bhumi one is able to simultaneously manifest one hundred nirmanakayas for the benefit of beings. There are eleven other such sets of one hundred abilities. For details see the *Abhisamayalamkara* by Maitreya.

TWO ACCUMULATIONS (tshogs gnyis) The accumulation of merit and wisdom.

TWO KAYAS (sku gnyis) Dharmakaya realized for the benefit of self and rupakaya manifested for the welfare of others.

TWO RUPKAYAS (gzugs sku gnyis) Sambhogakaya and nirmanakaya.

TWOFOLD KNOWLEDGE (mkhyen pa gnyis) The wisdom of knowing the nature as it is and the wisdom of perceiving all that exists. Knowledge of conventional and ultimate phenomena.

TWOFOLD PURITY (dag pa gnyis) Inherent or primordial purity and the purity of having removed all temporary obscurations.

UDUMBARA FLOWER (skt.) Literally "especially eminent" or "supremely exalted"; said to appear and bloom only accompanying the appearance of a fully enlightened buddha.

UNCHANGING ABSOLUTE ('gyur med yongs grub) Synonymous with emptiness or suchness. *See also* Three natures.

UNCONDITIONED DHARMADHATU (chos dbyings 'dus ma byas)

UNDERSTANDING, EXPERIENCE, AND REALIZATION (go myong rtogs gsum) Intellectual comprehension, practical experience, and unchanging realization.

UNELABORATE CONDUCT (spros med kyi spyod pa) One of the various types of enhancement.

UNFABRICATED NATURALNESS (ma bcos rang babs)

UNITY OF THE TWO KAYAS (sku gnyis zung 'jug)

UNIVERSAL LIGHT (kun tu 'od) The eleventh bhumi and the state of buddhahood according to the sutra system.

UNOBSTRUCTED NATURE (gdangs dgag med) One of the three aspects of the sugatagarbha: essence, nature, and expression.

UNSHAKABLE (mi g.yo ba) The eighth of the ten bodhisattva bhumis.

Glossary

Uttara Tantra (rgyud bla ma)   The "Unexcelled Continuity" by Maitreya. Translated and published as *The Changeless Nature* (Karma Drubgyud Darjay Ling, 1985) and as *Buddha Nature: Oral Teachings* by Thrangu Rinpoche (Rangjung Yeshe Publications, 1988).

VAJRA HOLDER (rdo rje 'chang)   *See* Vajradhara.

VAJRA VEHICLES (rdo rje theg pa)   *See* Vajrayana.

VAJRA VEHICLES OF THE RESULTANT SECRET MANTRA ('bras bu gsang sngags rdo rje theg pa)   *See* Secret mantra.

VAJRADHARA (rdo rje 'chang)   "Vajra-holder," the dharmakaya buddha of the New Schools. Can also refer to one's personal teacher of vajrayana.

VAJRALIKE SAMADHI (rdo rje lta bu'i ting nge 'dzin)   The final stage of the tenth bhumi which results in buddhahood.

VAJRASANA (rdo rje gdan)   The "diamond seat" under the bodhi tree in Bodhgaya where Buddha Shakyamuni attained enlightenment.

VAJRAYANA (rdo rje theg pa)   The "vajra vehicle." The practices of taking the result as the path. Synonymous with *secret mantra*.

VEHICLE (theg pa)   The practice of a set of teachings which "carries" one to the level of fruition.

VERY UNELABORATE CONDUCT (shin tu spros med kyi spyod pa)   A type of conduct for enhancement.

VICTORIOUS CONDUCT (rnam rgyal gyi spyod pa)   One of the numerous types of conduct.

VICTORIOUS ONES (rgyal ba, jina)   Synonymous with buddhas.

VIDYADHARA (rig 'dzin, knowledge-holder)   One who holds (dhara) or upholds the wisdom of knowledge (vidya)-mantra. An accomplished master of vajrayana.

VIPASHYANA (lhag mthong)   "Clear" or "wider seeing," one of the two main aspects of meditation practice, the other being shamatha.

WISDOM ESSENCE OF THE TATHAGATAS (de bzhin gshegs pa'i ye shes kyi snying po)   Synonymous with *sugatagarbha*.

107

Glossary

WISDOM OF ALL EXISTENT OBJECTS OF KNOWLEDGE (shes bya ji snyed pa [mkhyen pa]'i ye shes)   The aspects of the twofold knowledge which cognizes conventional phenomena.

WISDOM OF KNOWING THE NATURE AS IT IS (gnas lugs ji lta ba [gzigs pa]'i ye shes)   Perception of the ultimate truth.

YOGA OF NONMEDITATION (sgom med kyi rnal 'byor)   The fourth of the four yogas of mahamudra.

YOGACHARA (rnal 'byor spyod pa)   The mahayana school of philosophy established by Asanga.

YOGIC PRACTICES ('khrul 'khor)   Exercises utilized in the six doctrines of Naropa.